Everything Will
Be Okay

ALSO BY DANA PERINO

And the Good News Is...
Let Me Tell You About Jasper...

Everything Will Be Okay

Life Lessons for Young Women
(from a Former Young Woman)

~~~~~~

Dana Perino

TWELVE

New York   Boston

Twelve
Hachette Book Group
1290 Avenue of the Americas, New York, NY 10104
twelvebooks.com
twitter.com/twelvebooks

First edition: March 2021

Twelve is an imprint of Grand Central Publishing. The Twelve name and logo are trademarks of Hachette Book Group, Inc.

The publisher is not responsible for websites (or their content) that are not owned by the publisher.

The Hachette Speakers Bureau provides a wide range of authors for speaking events. To find out more, go to www.hachettespeakersbureau.com or call (866) 376-6591.

Library of Congress Control Number: 2020951081

ISBNs: 978-1-5387-3708-8 (hardcover), 978-1-5387-3707-1 (ebook)

Printed in the United States of America

LSC-C

Printing 2, 2021

For my mom, Janice M. Perino, the first to tell me that everything will be okay.

Contents

Introduction

I got a call from a young woman in Washington DC seeking some advice. She had a problem at work and was quite upset. Her office supervisor wanted her to do something that she was very uncomfortable with—make a public statement under her own name using language and a tone that she thought was disrespectful and unproductive.

"Then don't say it. Absolutely *do not* do it," I said.

"I don't think I can refuse," she said. She was afraid she'd be fired if she didn't comply, that she didn't have the gravitas to decline. "I'm not Dana Perino," she said.

"Well, how do you think I became Dana Perino?" I asked.

I'd had times in my career when I'd faced the same problem. I knew that pit of worry and fear that can make you nearly sick to your stomach when you think you're trapped or stuck (you're not!).

I suggested she rewrite the statement in her own words—if her name was going on it, then she had to take ownership of the opportunity.

You see, while she was worried that she was going to lose her job or be pushed aside, hurting her career plans, I had an alternative view—that if she didn't stick up for herself and do the right thing, the experience would chip away at her confidence and could hurt her career in a different way in the long run.

I told her that personal integrity is her *most valuable asset*—she had to fiercely protect it. And that suggesting the changes to the statement with dignity and grace would make her stronger the next time she confronted a challenge.

And the good news is...she rewrote the points in a way that made her feel comfortable *and* that satisfied her boss. Win-win.

Now—let's do you.

〰〰〰

CHAPTER 1

What Are We Doing Here?

The hardest part of any workout is the first step out the door—but if you make it to the gym, you're always glad you did.

It's the same with opening a book of advice.

So, congratulations! You made it to page 1.

I promise this will be worth your time (and you won't have to break a sweat!).

Ever since the spring of 2015 when I wrote *And the Good News Is…Lessons and Advice from the Bright Side*, the mentoring chapter is the one I am most often asked about when talking with young women.

I still get emails about my suggestion to stop wearing UGGs to work (and other tips for professional attire), that young women shouldn't shuffle around the office, seeming to be barely interested in their work. (*Pick up your feet!*)

I'm often credited for helping readers break the habit of overusing exclamation points(!!!)—doing so causes unnecessary panic and doesn't present an "I can handle this" image.

The advice on bigger-picture issues helped my readers, too—such as, not being afraid to move to a new town for work or other opportunities. And that choosing to be loved is not a career-limiting decision (and sometimes you should move *for* love ... but maybe not after one date).

Oh, and this one was memorable, too: Find your strong voice—and then use it wisely.

I'm grateful that my advice has apparently been helpful to quite a few people. That mentoring chapter packed a punch. And it was just a slice of the conversations I've had with and stories I've heard from so many young women who I've tried to help during the first phase of their careers.

Those early years are when you get your first job and love going to work every day. Then suddenly you grow out of that first position and can't wait to get on to your next role.

That's also when you're trying to decide what direction to go in and whether you even want to be in a particular industry or follow a certain profession. You may start questioning your choices from college—what you majored in may have been interesting but it may not have been a good choice for helping you reach your financial goals (yes, Dad, I know—I should have taken more business courses!).

Those early career days are when you start asking yourself, When should I leave a job? How do I move on without burning a bridge? How can the next move get me closer to achieving long-term goals?

You might notice that young men your age seem to get promoted sooner than young women—you think that's unfair but are unsure how to deal with it (trust me—taking up smoking cigars, going out for beers, or buying expensive golf clubs to try to fit in with them is *not* the answer).

The first few years can be exciting and fun, while also being confusing and difficult. Hey, they call it work for a reason.

And soon enough, you're making the transition from your first job to your second or third job. That's when—hopefully—everything starts falling into place. But that's also when the decisions you make begin to carry a lot more weight. The stakes are raised.

In your mid to late twenties, you gain more responsibility and you work much longer hours. It's also when you're trying to be taken more seriously and you may have to fight to be in the room for important meetings. You're not the boss yet—but you're also not a junior staffer anymore. You're expected to get results and earn your keep. The pressure builds.

And all of this is going on while you're trying to have an enjoyable personal life as well. You might be getting pressure from family or friends for working too much. You're wondering when you're going to meet a stable, responsible, goal-oriented, and attractive life partner who makes you laugh like crazy. You want to get a dog (but don't do it yet!). You want it all—and quickly. But you realize it is not happening as you imagined it would.

Your thoughts race. I'm even typing faster now.

How do I know what you're thinking?

Because not so long ago, I *was* you. I went through all of this. I made mistakes along the way—many, in fact. I wish I had this book when I was first starting out.

That said, everything turned out well. (I even got the dog.)

And here's what I want you to know. You're not alone in thinking or feeling the way you do. There are millions of young women in your age group that are trying to figure it out. Sometimes knowing that you aren't the only one with these worries can help. No—you're not crazy.

And I'm here to tell you there are ways to push through this period and come out happier and more fulfilled on the other side. There is no magic formula—if it were that simple, everyone would know what to do. But there are some basic—and important—things every young woman facing these decisions should know.

So why learn the hard way? As the book's subtitle says, I'm a former young woman myself. I've already made the mistakes. I've been through it.

Let me tell you what I learned:

I've always found career decision making fascinating, and I have an open door for young professionals who come to me for advice. (Guys come see me, too! A lot of this advice applies to everyone.) I try to help them feel better when they're leaving my office than when they entered. It almost always works.

But over the last couple of years, I've noticed something that's really started to bother me: the quarter-life crisis (that's age twenty-five or so) that I wrote about in 2015 is following young women well into their thirties and beyond.

This is how it usually goes: You've moved up from your first job, but you're not quite at the level you think you should be in terms of stature or compensation. You feel like you've done everything right. Your reviews from your supervisors are solid. You've brought a few good projects over the finish line. You don't wear UGGs to meetings or file your nails in the lunchroom. You're ready for your next step, but there's no position available that fits the moment.

You're facing an achievement gap—jobs you'd like to have require five to seven years of experience and you only have four. As a result, your résumé gets shuffled to the bottom of the pile. Your CV has the boss's coffee rings on it. It's sitting on her desk under three years of J.McLaughlin catalogues.

Meantime, you thought you'd have a house or family by now. Finding a life partner and having children feels very far off or even unreachable. Instead of feeling like you have momentum, you feel stuck. The most interesting thing in your life is a new Netflix series about some nut who lives with tigers. Nothing is turning out the way that you imagined it would. Dashed dreams fuel anxiety. Deep breaths and restful nights are harder to come by. While you try to maintain a positive attitude, you feel the pressure of time. Ticktock, ticktock.

Every day, the calendar reminds you that you're behind where you want to be or in comparison to your friends and peers (who, by the way, are having similar thoughts no matter what they say). You want to make a change, to be considered someone capable of doing more at the office, someone who would make a wonderful boss, a terrific wife, an amazing mother, and maybe even run for office one day. Or at least run an office one day. But everything feels on hold.

My concern: the temporary crisis threatens to settle into a way of life. And I'm alarmed you are so consumed by your worries that it's coming across as a lack of confidence and preventing you from living a joyful life. You want to pull the rip cord on your angst, but you're afraid that if you stop worrying, you won't achieve your goals. With this pattern, you'll never break out of the negative cycle.

Here's some good news: it doesn't have to be this way. This is a problem that can be solved. There are things you can do to break out of quarter-life-crisis mode.

There has never been a better time to be a young, educated woman in America. Being born in the United States means you've already won the lottery of life.

Let me tell you a story about how important and valuable your education is.

Several years ago, a friend of mine married a great guy: handsome, mature, funny—and an *actual* nuclear physicist! They wanted to try to adopt a child. Soon after the wedding, they signed up with an adoption agency, prayed that a baby would become a part of their lives, and waited for a call.

A few years went by and the phone didn't ring too much. They started to think it might not happen.

But before they lost hope, they tried one other adoption agency.

Fast-forward a few weeks. I'd called her to ask if she could participate in a mentoring event I was going to co-host in DC. She sounded rushed on the phone.

"I'd love to, but I'm frantically buying plane tickets to Florida. We've been chosen to adopt a baby. The mother is in labor, so we have to hurry," she said.

Hang up. Pack. Run to the airport. Fly. Experience a miracle. Become a mother.

Blessings abounded. The baby girl was healthy and the adoption was going smoothly. Still, the biological parents had ten days to change their minds and keep their child.

But they didn't. Instead, they suggested the two couples have dinner before they said good-bye. My friend's parents, who lived in Florida, volunteered to watch over their new granddaughter that evening. As they headed to the dinner, they were nervous. What would they talk about? How would it go? Would it be okay? They weren't sure they could fully express their gratitude.

Over the meal, my friend's husband asked the biological father, "What made you choose us?"

The answer: education.

The father said he watched the video my friends had made for the adoption agency a few times. In it, they showed their home, the neighborhood parks, and their favorite place to walk on Saturdays to get fresh fruit, vegetables, and flowers. Lots of the videos from other prospective parents were similar.

But there was something in their video that stood out from the others he'd seen.

Toward the end of it, my friend's husband said into the camera, "And we will do everything we can to send her to college."

And that was it.

"I realized that I could never send her to college. And that will make such a difference for her," he said.

College—think about what that meant to them and what they were willing to do to ensure their daughter could get the education she needed to succeed in life.

Now, I'm not saying everyone needs to go to college; there are lots of different paths for people to take in life—that's true. And many of today's collegiate paths lead to some pretty, um, odd places. (Try avoiding a major in Bigfoot studies.) But everyone needs to be educated in order to succeed. And by far, college attendance correlates to increased opportunity and more wealth accumulated over a lifetime.

Consider this—according to Georgetown University's Center on Education and the Workforce, someone earning a bachelor's degree will be worth more than $2.8 million on average over a lifetime. And they'll earn 31 percent more than people who get an associate degree, and 84 percent more than people graduating from high school with no additional education. This is why so many parents want their children to go to college. (That doesn't mean it has to be Ivy League—hey, look at me…no Ivy here! Only go to an Ivy League school if you can afford it and want to major in comedy writing. Their sports teams will give you all the material you need. My colleague Greg Gutfeld did this, but they made him the mascot. That's where he got those sweaters he wears on *The Five*.)

In the chapters ahead, you'll find practical advice that you can immediately use to improve your day-to-day work experience. I'll give you some tips taken from my own time as a young staffer to my time now as an observer of younger people, lurking in windows and storefronts as I do on the occasional windswept evening.

Think of me as your manager and your mentor, representative of the Generation X bosses out there. In time, you'll be the top dog, but until then, these pointers can immediately help you at work.

We'll also tackle how to answer some of the biggest questions you have, providing new ways to look at your career and your life. (Trust me—you're not the first person who wondered if leaving a sushi roll in her cubicle desk drawer for two weeks could be career ending. I assure you it could.)

And we'll talk about relationships and the important things you can do to build upon love and commitment—and finding someone to share all of it with—because in a few years (or right this minute!) you'll very much want that. Especially after a couple of Aperol Spritzes and a Ryan Gosling double feature.

I don't have all the answers, but here's some good news: you already have the solutions to the problems you're trying to solve. You already have everything you need. It's all inside of you, waiting to be tapped. All I'm going to do is help you turn on the spigot. And yeah, that's a gross metaphor. But who cares? We'll be going through it together.

You've got this.

‿‿‿‿‿

CHAPTER 2

Who Is Dana Perino Anyway?

For many of you, this might be the first time you're ever hearing of me or reading something I wrote. You may have been given this book by someone who loves you—a parent or grandparent, an aunt or uncle, a boyfriend or girlfriend, or maybe even a boss or mentor. I imagine if you aren't into politics or don't watch cable news, you may have no idea who I am. Therefore, you may be wondering, Why in the world should I read a book of advice by Dana Perino?

Allow me to introduce myself. I'll make this relatively quick—but the story of my life and career path will give you a better sense of who I am. And I'll provide some of the key foundational advice that I learned along the way.

So:

Today I anchor *The Daily Briefing with Dana Perino* on Fox News Channel, and I'm a co-host on the panel show *The Five*. I'm grateful to be on the election coverage team, to have had a podcast with my co-host Chris Stirewalt called *I'll Tell You What*, and to host *Dana Perino's Book Club* on Fox Nation.

I'm married to a British-born now American citizen, Peter McMahon (much more on this guy in a bit). Yet one of the reasons many people follow me is because they love my dog, Jasper. He's a Hungarian vizsla, the second of that breed Peter and I have raised. Years ago, on a show called *Red Eye*, I said I'd share my dog with everyone and nicknamed him "Jasper, America's Dog." Ever since, Jasper has had his own fan club and sometimes people stop us just to get a photo with him. (I'm not jealous...)

So, with a supportive husband in Peter and a loyal companion in Jasper, I find myself at forty-eight, doing everything I ever wanted to do in a career—it just took me a while and a circuitous route to get here.

Along the way, I had the best opportunity of my life—to be the first woman to serve as the White House press secretary in a Republican administration.

It all began in Wyoming (go Cowgirls!). I might be the only person you've ever "met" that came from the Equality State (so named because it was the first to grant women the right to vote in 1869).

My mom, Janice Marie Brooks, grew up in Rawlins, Wyoming (a small, dusty, and windy town with a strong neighborly feel). If you ever drive across the country, you'll likely take I-80 and go right through it. My mom's parents were entrepreneurs and ran the Uptown Motel when I was a kid.

My grandfather, Thomas R. Brooks, served in the army in Europe during World War II. My grandmother Dorothy "Dot" H. Brooks was a riveter in Denver (she even looked like Rosie). They married as soon as he got home from the war, and they honeymooned by road-tripping to Niagara Falls. My mom was the firstborn, and her little sister is my aunt Patty Sue Schuler (APS for short).

Growing up, my sister and I spent time with my grandmother after my grandfather died. I loved her homemade meals—pot roasts, potatoes and carrots, and cherry pies. She let us pick the marshmallows out of the Lucky Charms box of cereal. We could paint our nails garish colors. She had Jergens rose lotion in her bathroom and White Shoulders perfume on her dressing table.

We played a lot of card games, and she taught us to knock when our turn was over. We watched *Wheel of Fortune* as we sat in her big recliners, and when the news came on, she'd often say, "That Ronald Reagan sure does have a beautiful head of hair."

My dad, Leo Earnst Perino, was born in Rapid City, South Dakota—about eighty miles east of my grandparents' ranch in Newcastle, Wyoming. My great-grandparents emigrated from Italy, made their way to Wyoming, and homesteaded there in the Black Hills in the late 1800s. Over time, the ranch grew to be quite a large outfit and my uncle Matt Perino, his wife, Donna, and their sons and grandkids run it today.

I spent every summer and most holidays up there at the ranch. It is, by far, the place of my happiest childhood memories. It's where I learned the things that really matter—the importance of faith, family, character, honesty, patriotism, hard work, and fun.

It's also where I learned to bottle-feed a calf, ride a horse (starting with the pony my grandfather got me when I was a toddler—Sally), watch out for snakes, pick eggs, and enjoy a ride in the back of a pickup truck with the dogs as our pals. I came to appreciate fresh air, pine trees, rain after a dry spell, fresh tomatoes and cucumbers, and my grandfather's salad dressing of white vinegar, olive oil, salt, pepper, paprika, and a little bit of sugar. I don't get back to the ranch often enough, and I'm grateful they welcome me with open arms whenever I can visit. In many ways and in certain moods or moments, this is who I feel I really am—a cowgirl who "went east."

My parents moved to Denver, Colorado, when I was just over two years old. We lived in a small three-bedroom house. My sister, Angie, arrived two years later. While I was apparently very upset that I was kept home from school the day she was born, I came to adore her, and to this day she's my very best friend. We had a dog named Joco and a few cats along the way. (I still cringe when I think of my dad finding out we'd snuck home a kitten from the ranch one summer. He threatened not to let us keep her, but she got to stay, thankfully. We're sorry about that, Dad!)

For our early education, we walked to Ellis Elementary School (go Roadrunners!), and then we moved out to a more rural area, Parker, now a gigantic suburb that I barely recognize. They still have the old Pizza Hut, though, and I have fond memories of nights when my parents surprised us and said, "Let's go out tonight," and we'd get to go have dinner and play Pac-Man and Asteroids until the food arrived. Parker Junior High and Ponderosa High School were laid out so that you could see the Rocky Mountains and marvel that you got to live in that beautiful setting. I was on the speech team and the student council.

My sister and I had happy childhoods. We were loved and cared for. We had a lot of friends. And my parents worked hard to ensure we had good educations. My mom helped nurture us along the way, making sure we could take care of ourselves while knowing she was there if we needed her. She was a great role model.

Lesson alert #1: READ all you can and all the time

Education started at home. I learned to read early on, and my mom would struggle to keep me in books. I would read two library books in the back seat of the car by the time we got home—and we could only check out seven books at a time. So, I would just read them over and over again.

One time when we went to Target, my parents let me stay in the book section while they did the shopping. When they came to get me, I'd already read *Otherwise Known as Sheila the Great* by Judy Blume. I asked if we still had to buy it. My parents said yes, we did. With their example of making sure authors get paid for their work, I still buy books and subscribe to multiple news outlets.

I can point to one specific thing my dad did with me that helped me have the career I have today. When I was in third grade, he assigned me to read the *Rocky Mountain News* and the *Denver Post* every day before he got home from work (I loved assignments!). I had to choose two articles to discuss with him before dinner. He would ask me lots of questions about why I made my selections, what I thought of the stories, and then he'd debate other points of view that should be considered. Of all the things that helped in the communications business, this was probably the most important. For those of you who are contemplating (or experiencing!) parenthood, I'd say it's something worth considering—even in our digital age.

We were a newsy family. We got all the magazines and my dad and I would dog-ear pages and circle articles we wanted to discuss with each other later. As a family, we always watched the evening news and my parents set the alarm clock on the stove on Sunday evenings, because I had to come in from playing in the backyard in time for *60 Minutes* (what we could have done with a DVR in those days!). When I was asked, "What do you want to be when you grow up?" I would say, "News anchor." I never wavered on that. It was my plan.

Fast-forward. After getting good grades in high school and competing on the forensics team (speech and debate, not *Law & Order* / *CSI*), I took my dad's advice and applied to a smaller school over the big one I wanted to go to (you know, the kind with the football team, the sororities, and the parties). University of Southern Colorado (now CSU-Pueblo) is where I landed for college with a full-ride scholarship. I worked at the PBS television station on campus—producing shows, even hosting one (burn the tapes!). From there I went to graduate school at the University of Illinois-Springfield and studied public affairs reporting.

Lesson alert #2: If there's one thing you should absolutely focus on improving while you're in college or landing that first job, it's your writing style

I learned a lot in grad school about news writing. I'll never forget when all eighteen of us in the program failed our first writing assignment. We were shocked and embarrassed. But the professor was correct—we didn't write well. He needed to get us to a professional level and quickly. Over those months, and after all that schooling (K–12, college, and graduate school), we finally became better writers.

I wish that I'd focused more on writing when I was in college or that I'd had tougher instruction, because I really had to do a lot of catching up. I was a little ashamed that I didn't have better writing skills—again that feeling of inadequacy. You might feel that way, too. Well, there's no shame in working on getting better at something so important, especially when it comes to communications and writing.

Employers should not have to be the training ground for good writing, though in my experience, that's more often the case than not.

How can you set yourself apart from the get-go when it comes to your peers? Having better writing skills is key. Once you have greater competence in writing, a lot of other things, like promotions and more responsibility at work, fall into place. It's an important part of making sure that everything will turn out well for you.

If this is an area you need to focus on, there are many books written about writing (I love to read those), and they are worthy of your time.

Some of my favorites:

On Writing Well, by William Zinsser
The Elements of Style, by William Strunk Jr. and E. B. White
Eats, Shoots & Leaves, by Lynne Truss
This Is the Story of a Happy Marriage, by Ann Patchett

There are also several podcasts on writing that I like, including these:

Grammar Girl Quick and Dirty Tips for Better Writing
Write about Now, with Jonathan Small
A Way with Words, with Martha Barnette and Grant Barrett
Mad Dogs & Englishmen, with Kevin Williamson and Charles
    C. W. Cooke (this isn't a podcast about language, but their
    command of English is incredible)

Investing in improving your ability to communicate with the written word will pay dividends for the rest of your career. Besides, one day you'll have to help a young new staffer learn how to write better for your workplace. Let them see how you edit documents, and consider something I've found very helpful—I will copy or forward to junior staffers emails that I've written to colleagues or higher-ups, so they can see how I like it done.

My goal is to write messages that are so thorough and clear that no one is left confused or with follow-up questions. If my staff can do the same, we'll have less miscommunication and more productivity.

It takes time to write well at first, but once you have the hang of it, you'll find it comes naturally.

Back to the bio:

In graduate school I also learned something very valuable— what I did *not* want to do. Even though being a local anchor had been my career dream for as long as I could remember, I came to the realization that it wasn't for me.

My reluctance had been building for a while. While I really liked covering the state capitol and the political news of Illinois during my second semester of the master's degree program, the legislature wasn't in session for long stretches so I covered other news as well.

One day I was sent to cover some tornado damage, and I found I didn't really know how to tell the story as well as it needed to be told. Even my coverage of Garth Brooks's visit to a local factory that made his CDs and tapes felt awkward (it could have been the bolo tie I wore—facepalm emoji!). If it wasn't politics, I just didn't seem to have the knack... or the interest.

Plus, I wasn't great at editing video—the technology at the time was difficult for me to figure out. And many local stations were going to models where the reporters were one-man bands—shooting, editing, and writing everything in the field themselves. That just didn't appeal to me as much as I thought it would.

And there was something else I noticed. I was surprised by what I finally realized was a bias against conservative viewpoints. This happened in morning editorial calls, assignment decisions, and commentary around the newsroom. I knew it wasn't fair—but a lot of things aren't fair. It was eye-opening to say the least.

All of this took place over six months and reached a make-

or-break moment where I choked on a story—big-time. I'd been assigned to get an interview with the mother of a murdered child. At the courthouse, I circled her three times but couldn't bring myself to approach. I finally said to the cameraman that I wasn't able to do it. I couldn't interrupt her in that moment. Looking back, I realize she may have *wanted* to tell her story. And that my empathy isn't something that should prevent me from doing a job that I was assigned to do. But I was only twenty-two and just didn't have enough life experience to handle it with the strength and grace the moment required.

And that was the day I realized maybe the role of reporter isn't for me. Besides, the path to success in local news is quite arduous, with little pay and obstacles to get to the anchor chair. The window for success felt like it was narrowing as I finished graduate school, when I'd expected the opposite.

Plus, at the time, the three main networks all were anchored by the same three men I'd been watching since I was a kid. How could I get ahead?

I started to question my choices. Maybe my plan was wrong—which was a hard pill to swallow since I'd taken out quite a hefty student loan to pay for graduate school.

Lesson alert #3: Changing course is to be expected, not avoided. Embrace the change.

I went back to Colorado to reassess. I waited tables and lived in my parents' basement. I'd call a toll-free number for MediaLine, which was a listing of broadcast journalism jobs available across the country and how you looked for reporter jobs before the Internet. (Thank you, Vice President Gore, for inventing the Internet! This is a joke, BTW . . . google it.)

It was fun to listen to the listings and imagine living in Eugene, Oregon; Tucson, Arizona; Tallahassee, Florida; and even Guam. (I actually applied for a job on the US military base there, but when my dad and I happened to watch a PBS documentary on the brown tree snake infestation in Guam, I withdrew my name from consideration. No, thank you!)

I called MediaLine every day. I applied here and there. I was getting anxious and a little desperate. I quite liked waiting tables at Govnr's Park Tavern and made good money there. But time was poking me in the back like a sharp stick. I had to get a move on.

I didn't plan to go into government. It wasn't even on my radar. But I saw an ad for a deputy press secretary job with one of the leaders of the Colorado state legislature, a Republican. He was looking for someone with media experience and...well, I figured I had enough experience to get my foot in the door.

I wasn't likely to get a call back if I didn't have someone willing to vouch for me. I needed a good reference and I remembered Scott McInnis, a former state representative turned US congressman, who I used to interview on a show called *Capitol Journal* back at PBS. McInnis was always willing to take my questions and generous when he didn't have to be—our viewing audience wasn't that big and I was just a very green reporter in outfits from Casual Corner's Petite Sophisticate (your moms will know what I'm talking about).

I got up the nerve to call McInnis's office to see if I could list him as a reference on my application. His chief of staff was quick to say yes. But she had another idea in mind. She asked me if I was looking for a job, and would I consider coming to work for them? I started backpedaling—I didn't want to move back to Pueblo, Colorado.

Lesson alert #4: Always hear someone out—don't be hasty to turn down opportunities

However, the job she had in mind wasn't in the congressman's district office in Pueblo...it was in Washington DC. Now that...that sounded a bit more like it. Like a path with a possible future. It was a long way from home—and a real departure from my dream of working in the news business. But maybe that's just what I needed (fact check: true!).

The congressman's job opening was for a staff assistant position. In that role, you answer phones, sort the mail, greet visitors to the office, and give constituents tours of the Capitol. These tasks sounded easy; the move across the country and complete change in career direction—that was a little more daunting. Okay, a lot more.

I didn't accept the job right away. I had two concerns—the main one was that if I abandoned my plan to be in local news, then I would never get to work in television. Seriously, at twenty-three years old, that's what I thought. The second worry was that I didn't know anyone, literally not a soul, in Washington DC. How would I even begin to start in a whole new place?

I could list a lot of reasons not to take the job. But still, there was the nagging feeling that not following through on a career in media meant I had failed.

And to be honest, I was quite intimidated by others who had gone to "better" colleges than me. I wasn't an Ivy League graduate. I didn't go to a school that had a big social scene or an active alumni association that would help guide me. I wasn't sure I would fit in, or that I could cut it.

But the opportunity was knocking on my door. They wouldn't wait forever to fill a staff assistant position.

"Final answer?" I still couldn't decide.

So, I prayed about it, as I was taught as a child. And I put that prayer in the tiny moment of time between wakefulness and falling asleep (a little pocket), which I'd heard (apologies to the pastor of my Lutheran church) on the *Oprah Winfrey Show* was a great way to help make decisions.

Lesson alert #5: Reach back to what your parents taught you about religion and faith—it will help you over and over throughout your life

And sure enough, I woke up the next morning refreshed and with the calm that comes after making a tough decision. I was going to Washington DC.

A couple of weeks later, my mom, my aunt Patty Sue, and I drove across the country. Back through the fields of Kansas my dad and I had driven through when he picked me up from graduate school, past the horse farms of Lexington, Kentucky, where the white fences looked so pretty, and finally inside the Beltway where the Washington Monument and the Capitol dome served as beacons to our destination.

We made it. We parked the car in a spot five blocks from the Capitol near the room I'd be renting. Then I didn't drive it for five weeks—I was intimidated by the traffic in the city. (I got over it by taking the congressman's advice to get up early one Saturday morning and drive around getting used to the place. It worked.)

And from there, my career took off.

A month after being in Washington, I went to a hockey game (I knew nothing about the game, but the ticket was free). I sat next to someone who asked what I wanted to do in Washington. I replied that I wanted to work my way up to being a House press secretary one day (note: I didn't say the White House...just the congressional house, for a member of Congress). He just happened to know of such a job in another Colorado congressman's office. He said I should go for it.

I was hesitant.

"Wouldn't it look bad to change jobs so quickly? I just got here," I said.

"Oh, you have no idea how this works," he said.

The next day, he set up an interview for me with the outgoing press secretary on the fifth floor of the Rayburn House Office Building. She told me all about the job and sized me up, and went on to recommend me for the job.

And just like that, I joined Rep. Dan Schaefer's office. There I met my first real mentor, Holly Propst. Without her, I would not be the me of today. She taught me how to write (yes, I still needed to improve), brief a boss, manage a team, answer press calls, organize media events, and how to learn the policy rather than just pretending to understand the issues.

Everything was going so well. I had taken the leap, and it was working.

And yet, a couple of years into the job, I still went through the quarter-life crisis.

I felt like my long-held plans for my life weren't working out. I was ready for more responsibility, but there was no clear place to jump for a promotion. I wasn't even sure I wanted to do media relations anymore (reporters can be a pain in the rear—and now I am one).

I wondered if I should head out to California to work in the burgeoning tech industry. Or join the Peace Corps and see more of the world. I had no prospects for a husband—I didn't even have dates. There was no way I was going to make my goal of having two children, with a cute home in a good neighborhood, with secure finances and, I assumed, no real worries in the world.

I had a hard time snapping out of it until one of my friends at my church's singles group said, "Dana, remember what Jesus says: 'Fear not.' And he means it. Everything is going to be okay. Let God work his plan and let go of yours."

I remember this conversation like it was yesterday. I took her advice to heart. And over the next few weeks, I felt the clouds start to lift. My anxiety lessened. I was free from worrying about what was next for me for a while.

Keep this in mind when someone sends you a text and says they heard of a great job that you might be perfect for—but it is in a different field, a new town, or not part of your plan. If you read the life stories of successful people you admire, often you'll find that somewhere along the way they zigged when they thought they were going to zag, but that someone in their life presented the opportunity to them. My motto: Keep your eyes and ears open at all times. Consider any challenge an opportunity. Never dismiss something out of hand (unless we're talking about snake handling or fire juggling or something like that).

Lesson alert #6: Choosing to be loved is not a career-limiting decision

So, there I was just going about my business, focusing on my career, totally chill about finding a boyfriend, about to get on an airplane when...I met my future husband, Peter McMahon (this is a true story).

I almost missed the flight—my sister and I misjudged the distance to the airport, and I ran through the terminal to make it. Peter almost took an earlier flight because he was up and ready to go. We were the last two to hand over our tickets. He said he'd hoped we would be seated together. We were. What were the chances? (Side note: In writing this book, I asked Peter why he'd wanted to sit next to me. He said, "Why does any guy want to sit next to a pretty girl on a plane?" So, he didn't immediately want to marry me. That idea took another two hours into our flight to form.)

He asked me if he could put my bag up above, and I heard his British accent and was intrigued. Did a quick scan—no wedding ring. Book reader. John Le Carré's *The Tailor of Panama*.

"How do you like that book?" I asked.

From there, we talked for the two and a half hours from Denver to Chicago. He was well traveled, well spoken, well mannered, well dressed, well everything (except that he brought a McDonald's Filet-O-Fish...on an airplane! That could have been a deal breaker).

He was staying a night in Chicago. He asked me to go have a coffee, but I had a connecting flight to DC.

There were lots of reasons it was impossible to imagine that we'd ever be able to be together. Peter's British and lived in England at the time. He's eighteen years older than me—which seemed like quite a bit when I was twenty-five and he was forty-three. Did I mention he lived in England? I had a career and a plan, you know!

We corresponded on email and with letters. I rushed home to get them—it was quite romantic.

Six weeks after the plane ride, we had our first date in New Orleans. A week later he came to Washington DC and while there asked me to marry him.

"Hold that thought. Let me get my bearings," I said.

Because this was most definitely not in my plan.

Ah, to heck with the plan.

Just a few months later, I moved to the UK, and we got married soon after that. I couldn't work because I didn't have a visa, so I volunteered a bit and read a ton of British news and historical fiction. We got a puppy—Henry the vizsla—who became quite famous over the course of his life. All that time, I was loved and cared for like I never imagined. And he and I could never have dreamed of what would happen next.

After nearly a year, we moved back to the USA. Peter loves America. I mean he *really* loves it. Take any American event, and he will cheer the loudest—he can get choked up at a Fourth of July BBQ. We had no jobs and no concrete plans, so we could live anywhere in the country. We decided on San Diego because who wouldn't want to live in one of America's best vacation spots?

Looking back, I can hardly believe we did it the way we did. Peter was going to start a business, and I'd look for a job. We got a one-bedroom apartment and didn't even own a mattress when we arrived. But we had a lot of love and a bit of money we borrowed from Peter's friend and previous boss.

Surprisingly, it rained for the first five months we were in San Diego (this was not as advertised), but we barely noticed. I taught Peter how not to agonize over the menu at our favorite Mexican restaurants. (Burrito? Enchilada? Tostada? "Basically, Peter, it's all the same ingredients with different wrappers." He got it after that.)

In San Diego, I found work in public relations and had clients in the tech industry. To be honest, most of them were jerks. I remember this one guy who was mad at me that he wasn't on the front page of the *Wall Street Journal*. I explained that without a bigger hook, that wasn't going to happen. And he said to me, "Dana, who is the boss of you? It is me. That's who." As I was flipping him off into the phone, I knew right then that I wanted to be my own boss one day.

It didn't take too long before I was listless. I didn't see the way to get ahead in the business there. And I didn't really like working at a public relations agency.

I wanted more. I wanted to do something that mattered (and that didn't include getting some sillyproduct.com business an article in the paper to get more venture capital funding).

What I really wanted to do was to work for President George W. Bush. I had reluctantly turned down a volunteer opportunity to work on his 2000 campaign because I needed my job (with its benefits) while Peter got his business going. When I hung up the phone with his campaign, I cried, "Now I'll never get to work for George Bush." (Wrong again!)

Peter knew that a bored Dana is not a good Dana, so he said we should explore a change. I was worried he'd be disappointed about leaving San Diego, but as you'll see, Peter is the best.

One night he got out his whiteboard (we call this "The Whiteboard Incident") and asked me to list all the things I wanted to do in a job. Then he made another column of all the things I didn't want to do. And when we tallied it up, any job in Washington DC was better for me than any job in San Diego. In that moment, we set our sights on a possible move. So the result: not only did a relationship not *hinder* my career . . . but it also *helped* it.

Soon after, we woke up to the news of the 9/11 terror attacks. My God.

The terrorist attacks on September 11, 2001, changed everything. So much grief, anger, and fear. There was life before that dark day and then life after. It was a shocking inflection point that stirred the United States to fight back against an evil ideology that sought the destruction of western civilization.

As President Bush said, America didn't choose this fight. But she will win it.

Lesson alert #7: Stay in touch with your people

That horrific event changed the course of my life, too.

Following 9/11, I had been in touch with a friend from my Capitol Hill days, Mindy Tucker. In 2001, she was the director of communications for the attorney general. I sent her an email asking if she was okay. She called me a couple of days later. Would I be willing to come back to Washington? She needed another spokesperson on her team. I started packing right then.

Peter stayed behind and readied our tiny new house to be rented. I got to DC and moved back into my old English basement apartment that had become part of the house of my good friend Desiree Sayle. Desiree already worked at the White House in the correspondence office and was the mother of two daughters—a newborn and a toddler. I helped them where I could (which meant watching *Toy Story 2* a lot...Okay, all the time) while Desiree worked exceedingly long hours, and I waited for my clearance to start at the Justice Department.

Not long after I joined DOJ, I was in meetings with the team from the White House Council on Environmental Quality (CEQ). Before the year was out, I joined CEQ as the director of communications. I handled the press calls and communications events for energy and environment issues so that everyone else in the White House press office could focus on anti-terrorism efforts, the economy, education reform, and everything else that came their way.

Lesson alert #8: Always take the deputy job if it's offered to you. You may work weekends and holidays, but that's where you learn to do the job well and get face time with the boss.

In January 2005, I started as the deputy White House press secretary under Scott McClellan. The other deputy was Trent Duffy. We divvied up the issue areas—I kept energy and environment and added the Justice and Homeland Security Departments. I stayed on as the late (and wonderful) Tony Snow became the press secretary. We worked hard. Very hard. As my friend at the National Security Council would say on Friday nights as we walked out of the West Wing together, "We have long days and short weeks." Time flew.

And though all of us were under tremendous stress and strain, and we fought with the media every day while also trying to answer their questions and get the president's message out, we were joyful. Every day.

President Bush promoted me to be his press secretary in late August 2007.

I almost resigned right before I got the job. Divine intervention prevented that from happening.

That summer of 2007, Peter and I talked a lot about how much longer I would stay at the White House.

I was tired. *Really* tired. I wasn't sure I could give it my all through 2008. The job was all consuming, and he and I really wanted our time together to be restored. I had knots in my stomach as I walked into work that day. I said a prayer of gratitude as I did every time the United States Marine opened the door to the West Wing. I went to the communications meeting, and the president's counselor, Ed Gillespie, asked if he could see me after the meeting.

"Sure, I need to see you, too," I said. I was nervous as a cat—I didn't want to say the words that I was going to leave.

I don't know why, but thank God Ed said, "Can I go first?"

"Please, go ahead," I said.

"The president would like to make you the press secretary this Friday."

Um...what?

It wasn't a line one hears very often. Thank goodness I was sitting down. A million thoughts raced through my head—the first one being *OMG YES* and the second was *Oh no, poor Peter!*

Instead of telling Ed that I'd planned to resign that morning, I calmly said, "I'm honored. What do we need to do to get ready?"

I knew right then that President Bush had changed my life forever.

Without his trust in me, I wouldn't have been able to push my boundaries and to do a daily press briefing, manage my team, and handle multiple crises at once all while trying to maintain as much grace as I could muster.

One of the questions I'm most often asked is how I kept my composure at the podium in front of the combative press corps. Well, I knew I didn't want anyone to see me stumble or sweat when answering questions or making points. Every day I thought, *If President Bush is watching this right now, would he be proud of me? Would he agree with how I'm presenting his decisions? Would he think I am representing him well?*

Those questions kept me grounded. I also swallowed all my sarcastic responses. (But let them loose in the postbriefing get-together in my office where we'd let off some steam and say, "Imagine if I'd said..." These will go in my *Tweets I Never Sent* fantasy book, publication date TBD.)

Being the press secretary gave me an opportunity to be gracious under extreme pressure. I learned so much about the policies of health care, energy, education, and agriculture, as well as foreign policy areas from terrorism to trade to aid. I witnessed the tragedies of natural disasters, the heartache of families of wounded and fallen soldiers, and the triumph of newly sworn in citizens of the United States of America. I met everyday heroes and heads of state, got to listen to fascinating conversations between world leaders, and I even got to brief some of them.

I'll never forget my first briefing of a world leader other than President Bush. It was none other than the Russian president, Vladimir Putin. I was the deputy press secretary at the time. We were in Europe, and my job was to hang out with the reporters up until the press conference the two leaders would hold after their meeting. Before they took to their microphones, I would have to tell them what was on the media's minds and what questions they were likely to ask. And I was told that I'd need to remind Putin that our reporters would most likely ask about press freedoms in Russia.

I walked into the room. President Bush nodded at me and said, "What do you have?" I told him a few of the questions that would come up, and then I steeled my nerves, turned to meet Putin's cold blue eyes, and said, "And Mr. President, our press corps is likely to ask you about press freedoms in your country."

He waited a beat. And then he turned to President Bush and asked, "Why would I comment on press freedoms in my country when you just fired that journalist?"

Everyone looked confused.

"Vladimir, what are you talking about? I didn't fire any journalist."

"Yes, you did. You fired him."

President Bush then realized what Putin meant.

"Vladimir, are you talking about Dan Rather of CBS News? I didn't fire him. I *can't* fire him. His *company* fired him," he said.

"Yes, you did."

"Vladimir, I'm telling you—don't say that out there. That isn't true. I don't want you to be embarrassed."

Silence.

With that, I was given the nod by the president that I was free to leave. I was happy to go—I felt like I'd escaped a polar bear cage.

I took my seat in the press conference and watched the presidents take two questions each. Sure enough, the last question from our reporters had to do with the restrictions on freedom of speech and, sadly, the deaths of several journalists who had somehow "thrown themselves out of windows."

It was a good question. He had a terrible answer.

Putin said that President Bush had fired "that newsman." The reporters glanced at each other, trying to figure out what he was talking about. When it sunk in, I could see them shaking their heads and trying to stifle their giggles.

"That guy actually thinks President Bush fired Dan Rather?" they kept saying for the rest of the trip. Yep, he certainly thought that. He probably *still* thinks that.

In the last year of the Bush administration, we visited fifty-two countries. It was incredible. I learned so much along the way.

Out of all the trips, the one to Africa in February 2008 affected me the most. I was captivated. The potential of that continent is inspiring, but the poverty is devastating. It is a continent so rich in resources, with many loving people who just need a helping hand.

Peter and I would return to Africa in 2009, right after the inauguration of President Barack Obama, where we volunteered at a PEPFAR site and developed a strong commitment to helping where we could ever since.

I look back on my years at the White House with a deep and abiding fondness. Everything I did and learned there led me back to what I originally wanted to do as a kid—work in news, covering politics and, as a bonus, having a lot of fun.

And I've never forgotten what it felt like to be trusted with so much responsibility.

Lesson alert #9: Be grateful

You've got plenty to be grateful for—more than you realize. And here's something I believe: if you start to live with gratitude, your mood improves, you realize that there is a lot to be grateful for, and then more good things will come your way. You might consider starting a gratitude journal where you write down three things every day that you are grateful for. Think of it like gratitude karma—what goes around comes around (gratefully).

I took the lessons I learned from the White House into my career transition. It takes me aback when I hear people say that I seem to have handled it all so smoothly, that my career has been this steady climb, and that I never seem to get riled or frazzled.

That's really funny to me, because I don't remember it that way. I was a wreck a lot of the time. Though I guess I hid it well. But masking your anxiety doesn't work forever—it can crush you. Eventually, you have to make the decision to work through it. That takes effort, but there are tools you can use that can make it easier.

Looking back, I can tell you what helped pull me through.

First, my faith and my family. I was raised in a Lutheran household and have remembered to rely on my faith just when I think all is lost. When I feel overwhelmed, I recall the Bible verses that I memorized as a kid and then finally understood as an adult, such as "I can do all things through Christ who strengthens me" (Philippians 4:13 NKJV). Sometimes I will just repeat that sentence until

I'm calmer and more assured that I can handle whatever I'm dealing with. (It helps when dealing with the DMV as well.)

My mom and dad loved my sister and me unconditionally—and that's the key for raising kids who can learn how to take risks and become independent. We knew that if we screwed up or failed, they'd be there for us. The blend of faith and family really is a winning combination.

Second, my husband. I rely so much on Peter—one of the best listeners and most knowledgeable people I've ever known. So many people depend on him and feel better after they talk to him. He doesn't solve your problems—he helps you solve your own.

Third, my mentors. Let me tell you about a talk I had with the late Charles Krauthammer. Charles was the preeminent conservative columnist and commentator of my lifetime. I was honored to know him when I was at the White House and later at Fox News Channel. After Peter and I returned from Africa in 2009, Charles invited me to his office for some career counseling (for me, not for him).

It was awfully generous of him to give me that time. He asked me what I wanted to do. I told him of all my plans. He gently suggested that it sounded like it would be too much to start a public relations business, plus be a political analyst and TV personality. He reminded me that it wasn't possible, ethically, to be both a public relations professional with clients as well as a political commentator. He knew that there were inherent conflicts. Some people can handle both, but he knew that I'd feel conflicted and uncomfortable (he was right). Plus, he said, "If you go the PR route, you'll probably make a lot more money than if you stick with politics. But if you stick with politics, you'll have a lot more fun and enjoy your life better." He was right.

When Fox News invited me to be on *The Five*, at first I felt inundated because I was still running my business and trying to do as many Fox appearances as I could on the side. (Appearances on Fox were by far my favorite thing to do every day.) But when I finally settled in and when *The Five* became a permanent weekday show on the channel, I eventually let the PR business go. As soon as I did, I felt free from being pulled in too many directions. Right again, Charles! God, I sure miss him.

Since 2009, my roles and responsibilities have grown at Fox News. In October 2017, I was offered an opportunity to anchor my own news show, and we called it *The Daily Briefing with Dana Perino*. It's been a terrific challenge—we have been right in the thick of major news stories for several years, a global pandemic, a recession due to the pandemic, racial strife, a historic election, natural disasters, and the changing world of technology and the consequences of those advances for citizens, students, employers, and policy makers. Every morning I wake up feeling like I've been shot out of a cannon. It's a pace that suits me, and I have a team that is so smart I just want to buy a billboard for them in Times Square so that everyone knows how very good they are at their jobs (shout-out to the producers of both shows, led by Megan Albano).

I'm fulfilled from a career that I only dreamed about as a child. As a young adult, I felt inadequate, that I didn't have what it would take to make it to this level. Looking back, sure there were a lot of hard days, many challenges. Several times I wanted to give up and head back to something simpler. But then I'd have missed out on all the good stuff that came once I was through the quarter-life crisis and on to figuring out how to avoid a midlife crisis! (Still working on that... So far I've not bought a red convertible but I *have* thought about getting another Jasper!)

So, that's my background. And if you're still wondering why you should listen to me, consider this reason: because I care about you.

Lesson alert #10: Pay it forward

One of the best parts of getting a little older is being able to help younger people. You end up with a little success and suddenly people will ask you for advice—and you think, *Really? What do I know? I'm still trying to figure it out myself!* But every experience you have leads you along your life path—and if you can help someone avoid making a similar mistake or give them encouragement that everything will be okay, you'll get a ton of satisfaction by alleviating their worries.

In 2009 I had an idea to create a mentoring program that would be fun and efficient—like speed dating. That year I cofounded Minute Mentoring with Dee Martin, Susan Molinari, and Jamie Zuieback. It's been an awesome adventure. We host Minute Mentoring events in our spare time (not a lot of that!) and out of the goodness of our hearts. I've loved it.

Nothing makes me happier than seeing a young woman emerge from her quarter-life crisis, realize her potential, and see her hard work pay off.

I am invested in your success. Together, we will get you moving in the right direction and turn the page to an exciting new chapter in your life. (Seriously, turn the page, though—there's much more ahead.)

CHAPTER 3

What Is the Biggest Problem You're Trying to Solve?

Remember this:

You can't solve a problem you haven't defined.

Let's go back to those racing thoughts you may be having about your career (and maybe your love life—but let's focus on getting work right first).

An example sticks in my mind. I have a friend who took a big leap by leaving one very good job for the chance to try her hand in a related field (from TV production to political communications).

Her new job was less certain in its longevity, and when her boss lost an election, she was suddenly unemployed. I knew she'd be fine in the long run—she's an educated, outgoing, well-connected, and cheerful young woman. She's a good storyteller—a delight to be around.

I knew she was extremely tired from the pace and pressure of the campaign she'd worked on, and when your mind and body are craving rest, every problem feels bigger than it is. So, I called to ask how she was doing.

When she answered the phone, she launched into orbit. She spoke for a full five minutes without taking a breath, blurting out all her worries in one long sentence. She was so worked up that she imagined never getting another job, becoming destitute, and having to start all over. She was also worried about not getting any credit for the work experience she already had under her belt. As she circled back to where she began, I interrupted her.

"Stop. Just stop for a second. You sound frantic. Your mind is moving so fast that your mouth can't keep up. You don't sound like yourself. You're taking today's problems and turning them into tomorrow's disasters," I said. "You have to stop looking too far ahead."

I asked her to take some deep breaths. I stayed on the phone while she did. Then I asked her if she'd been sleeping. She hadn't. It was time for an intervention.

We talked it through, and I gave her some different ways of thinking about her situation. I suggested making a list of her concerns and then grouping them into things that weren't important, things that could be handled easily with a little time and effort, and things that appeared very difficult to solve.

What we found is that she was worrying too much about what had happened in the past at the previous job (slights by former colleagues, doing more than her fair share of work, not getting credit for successes but blamed for things that didn't go well, and so on). I suggested listing all of those hurts and worries and then burning the list in the fireplace. Those kinds of feelings happen in every job. She could let them go.

For the things she could stop worrying about by doing something about them, we made a plan. She'd dedicate an hour in the morning and the afternoon to do basic things like transferring her contacts to the cloud, updating her résumé and LinkedIn profile, and making three to six contacts with friends and colleagues to let them know she was back on the job market. By assigning herself a set of tasks, my highly motivated friend could get some control over stuff that was driving her crazy because she didn't know where to start.

And then we got to the big things. The "I don't know what I want to do with my life and what if I made a big mistake" kind of things. Aha. So that's what was *really* bothering her. All the other racing thoughts were just trying to bury the toughest questions she was wrestling with.

From there, we talked about how the biggest problems she was trying to solve were what she really needed to deal with—the other stuff was filler.

She took a few months to really think about what she wanted to do. She went on a lot of informational interviews. She utilized her network to talk to many different companies. And when she settled on one that she liked, she took the job and her career steamed ahead after that. She got promotion after promotion. And now her biggest problem has changed—now it's how she can manage the workload and responsibility as a boss in the C-suite. It's a good problem to have.

My friend and I talk almost every day. I love to watch her thrive in her executive role at one of America's largest companies. From time to time we revisit that panicked call—in hindsight, it's almost funny. Though she reminds me it wasn't funny at the time!

* * *

So, how would *you* answer the question *What is the biggest problem you're trying to solve right now?*

Perhaps you've never put it into words.

Your biggest problems sometimes feel so overwhelming that you're afraid to face them. You hope they'll disappear on their own.

Or maybe your biggest problem is so all consuming that you know exactly what it is. It keeps you up at night, follows you around all day, and won't listen when you tell it to go away. You might fill up your hours working on all the other problems you have, the ones that you feel you can handle or that are easier to solve, thinking that one of these days you'll tackle the big one.

But I'm here to break it to you—there's only one way to solve your biggest problem: identify and deal with it.

When I ask women what they're worried about, I better have some time on my hands. Women are very good worriers.

If I gave myself permission to list all my worries, I could start with things as small as finding time to get a manicure to wondering how I'll help take care of my mom and dad as they get older when I live so far away, to looking for a way to help reduce plastics in the ocean—and everything in between.

There is a strange comfort in worry—we've become accustomed to that feeling in our chest, where it is tight and it's hard to take a deep breath. It feels more natural to worry than to let worry go.

Worry is natural. It's part of our DNA, making us smarter about dangers so that we can survive. Worrying is an active way to try to predict what might happen next, and to plan what we'll do if the worst comes to pass. It gives us some feeling of control over the future (even though that's a mirage).

Instead of trying to solve all the problems you're worried about, it's more productive to pare it down and identify what the biggest problem is. Once you do that, you can start to solve it.

*   *   *

Knowing that I wanted to write this book, I needed to get a firm handle on what was really bothering young women today. I had a pretty good idea based on all the mentoring I do, but I wanted to focus. If I tried to address all the worries that young women have in this book, I'd never write, "The End," and we would have solved nothing by trying to solve everything.

To find out what was really on the minds of young women striving in their careers today, I threw a dinner party. I invited a group of ten young women (ages twenty-four to thirty-six) who worked in different fields to come over to my apartment one night for an evening with me and a co-founder of Minute Mentoring, Jamie Zuieback.

The ladies who came that night worked in a variety of economic sectors: technology (operations), social media (crisis communications), broadcast journalism, sales for a major mail-order subscription company, television production, and nonprofit management.

They came from a variety of backgrounds and experiences, including graduating from a military academy and serving in Iraq and Afghanistan; giving Nashville a try as a country music singer-songwriter before switching gears when that dream didn't come true; and moving to New York City and adjusting to the Big Apple. One was married, another getting over a recent breakup, and still another dealing with cultural pressures to only date and marry within her family's religion.

Everyone was going through something.

As we gathered that night to a dinner of green salad with Italian vinaigrette dressing, ravioli with Bolognese, and steamed vegetables, we made easy conversation getting to know each other better.

I'd asked my guests to bring an answer to the question *What is the biggest problem you're trying to solve right now?*

They came prepared. Some of the problems were the same ones I'd heard since starting Minute Mentoring, but their concerns had grown a bit. The problems seemed more mature, tougher to solve. Not wearing UGGs around the office wasn't going to fix these issues.

These young women had moved beyond their entry-level positions and had more responsibilities now. They were very focused, with a better sense of their career paths. Some were managing people for the first time and dealing with all of the challenges that come from the role as "the boss."

Their answers helped me decide what to include in this book, because I'm sure their concerns are shared by working women everywhere.

The problems they had to solve included the following:

- Wanting to be taken more seriously around the office (and as seriously as the guys at work)
- Managing expectation overload without adequate training
- Being asked to read minds—lack of clear guidance
- Wondering how to know when it's time to leave a job
- Feeling stuck in a role and wanting more while also being in what I call the "experience gap" (having four years of experience when the next step requires five to seven years)
- Needing to establish a work ethic, like a statement of purpose or personal code
- Establishing a competitive advantage, to be considered unique and not part of a crowd
- Dealing with an overwhelming amount of stress
- Finding a manageable work/life balance
- Finding time for family, friends, travel, and fitness
- Being true to oneself—even if cultural issues at home and the workplace make that difficult
- Wanting to be in a committed relationship and unsure how to find a life partner

As I'd seen in other Minute Mentoring events, having women share their concerns among other women of similar circumstances got everyone nodding along, because all of them were dealing with these big issues in one way or another at this point in their careers. When we got to "work/life balance" and some of the other topics, we looked like a room of bobblehead dolls, all nodding at the same time.

These young women were doing better in their careers—and this is true of young women across America—than previous generations in our country's history. In almost every field, women are succeeding more than ever before. Women are advancing rapidly, and yet they feel that time is not on their side. They're in a bit of a hurry to make something (and everything!) happen.

We talked through their problems, and they realized they weren't alone in their worries. They could share their concerns and shake the feeling that they were the only ones struggling to figure out how best to manage early adulthood. There's something special about women—how we can communicate with a glance, understand each other with just a look and a nod, speak entire paragraphs with just a little smile, make a case of wine disappear in record time . . .

Looking back to when I was going through my quarter-life crisis, I thought that I was the only one who couldn't get myself on track. As if I were the only young woman who wondered about her career path, worried she'd stayed too long in a job, or puzzled over how to meet a guy who I'd want to spend my life with.

What made a difference for me was sharing my worries and insecurities with a few trusted friends. By allowing myself to be a little vulnerable, I got good advice, learned from what they'd gone through, and could apply those lessons to my new outlook.

This is a pattern that repeats itself. When I got promoted to press secretary at the White House, I reached out to friends who understood that I felt overwhelmed and somewhat inadequate for the job. Turns out that nearly everyone feels that uncertainty when they're moving up the ladder. I picked up advice along the way. Here is some that I remember and that I've passed on to others:

- Don't try to do everything at once—you'll never catch up. So: *prioritize.*
- Listen way more than you talk at first—get a feel for how everyone thinks, what their strengths are.
- Find your allies and forge strong bonds with them.

- You're new—no one expects you to know everything, so use this time to your advantage.
- Avoid comparing yourself to your predecessors too much—embrace the opportunity and be yourself.
- Set boundaries early, such as best times to reach you when you're away from the office for a weekend.

This is also true for new mothers deciding how best to handle day care, daughters who are helping an elderly parent transition to assisted living, and moms with young adult children struggling to get a foothold after college. Talking things over with trusted friends or colleagues can relieve you of the burden of feeling that you're alone. And you might pick up some good tips that you can apply to help solve your problems. Think of it as a relief—you're not the first to have this problem, and you're not alone!

I believe this is something that we at Minute Mentoring found the most useful from our sessions. Sharing concerns and offering advice among a small group of people, where it was safe to be very open about their worries, gave people a lift.

And so that night at the dinner at my apartment, I witnessed it again. Here were these remarkable young women investing in themselves to improve, grow, or get unstuck. They had taken personal responsibility to focus on their futures and were dedicated to making good personal decisions. I knew that everyone there was likely to be very successful—and they'd be more likely to succeed if they continued to share their best practices or worst experiences with each other over their careers.

An overall observation of listening to all these young women was that the direction your life takes comes down to personal responsibility and making good choices.

Now, if you're reading this, you've already taken the first step toward self-improvement: self-reflection. That's good—because, honestly, no one else can do this for you. You must make smart choices.

Every day, we have to make thousands of decisions. Scratch that. We *get* to make thousands of decisions a day.

Being a responsible adult means making decisions—on everything—such as what to eat, whether to exercise, how to respond to a request, when to start a job search, whether to buy that new outfit, and whether you should go out tonight or stay home and get a good night's sleep. (The list goes on and on... including deciding what goes *on* the list!)

Having to make decisions isn't a burden. Getting to make decisions is a blessing. Try to reframe your thinking into what a gift it is to live in a free country where you have so many choices to make. What many women around the world would give to be in our position—lots of them have decisions made for them. Imagine living that way. I've seen it in many countries—it's not a way you'd want to live.

And a choice you get to make is how do *you* want to live? With intention and purpose? With joy? With determination? With love? Maybe you have big dreams and know exactly what you want to do. Or perhaps you are just not at all sure what you're good at or should be doing. You may be pressured to follow one path when your heart wants to go in a different direction.

Now is a great time to take stock of your life, of where you are, and to think about where you want to go and what it will take to get there. And to enjoy the journey along the way.

Take a moment here to create your own "Whiteboard Incident" to assess where you are right now. Here's a starter kit:

1. Get a whiteboard (ha).
2. Make two lists:
   - What responsibilities do you have in your current job that you really don't want to do?
   - What do you really want to do in a job?
3. Assign negative points to the answers in the first question and positive points to the second. Weigh the things you don't want to do in a job against those you *do* want to do. Then use those to balance your current job or career choice against a direction you'd like to take.

   If the negative points far outweigh the positive ones, it's obvious a change is needed. Either it's finding a different role within your company, looking to move on to another organization, starting your own business, or taking a class to learn new skills that would help you get the job you want.
4. Make one more list of jobs that you think you might like to have that would give you the opportunity to start doing the things you'd like to do. Start researching companies and reaching out to friends, alumni, and those willing to engage on platforms like LinkedIn to find out more.

Bottom line—if your score on your Whiteboard Incident adds up to you needing to make a change, then you have to take matters into your own hands and get going.

The Whiteboard Incident can be used again and again—even to evaluate personal relationships, or where you might want to live. Assess, reassess, take some time to think about it, and then act. Repeat.

The answers to these questions take time to find. Finding a mentor or a mentoring circle and starting the process is a great first step. The second? Finding someone you admire and learning how to be more like them. Role models—that's next.

〰〰〰

CHAPTER 4

How Do You Find a Role Model?

One of the best ways to figure out who you want to be and how you want to live is to observe others. We learn best by watching and listening, taking it all in.

Think about who you admire. Why are you drawn to her? Is it her strength, sense of humor, capabilities, determination, dignity, or grace? Perhaps it's the way she balances her career and family, or how she carries herself when under incredible pressure. Maybe it's how she broke a glass ceiling, proving the naysayers wrong. Or even how she never seems to get rattled—I'm a big believer in Dry Idea's motto: "Never let them see you sweat" (yes, that is a deodorant).

Whatever it is that makes you want to be like someone else, try to emulate her style and approach in your own way to become the best version of you. (Not a carbon copy of someone else—imitation is flattery but taken too far can be creepy!)

Role models change throughout your life—keep looking for them. I know I have. As a young girl, I admired my mother, aunts, godmother, and grandmothers. They helped shape who I am today. From a professional standpoint, I also looked to the careers of Diane Sawyer (from the Nixon White House to ABC News) and Mary

Hart (*Entertainment Tonight*—and she's from the Mount Rushmore State. South Dakota represent!). Fictional characters can also be role models: I think of Cybill Shepherd in *Moonlighting* as a spunky career woman who confidently wore white tennis shoes with her suits—that was fashion-forward in the 1980s (and like Hilary Duff in *Younger* in the here and now).

At the White House, my goodness, there were so many women I respected: First Lady Laura Bush, Secretaries Condoleezza Rice and Margaret Spellings, and Fran Townsend, to name a few. Finally, on to Fox News, where I have wonderful colleagues who keep teaching me the ropes. And I've witnessed Suzanne Scott work her way up to CEO of the company. With a steady hand, no drama, and little fanfare she's guided the company to new records for ratings and revenue. So, I've learned there are role models everywhere you look.

I want to highlight one in particular: Ann Gloag. She's a Scottish woman I found via an African journey by way of a Dallas fundraising dinner. How's that? Let me explain.

I mentioned how the presidential trip to Africa in 2008 was life changing for me. Well, even after Peter and I returned from our long trip to South Africa in 2009, I continued to want to help.

In 2010 I joined the women's advisory board for the ONE Campaign. Our goal was to provide support for women's and girl's education and to improve maternal and early childhood health.

That year I went with the ONE Campaign to three countries—Nigeria, Ghana, and Sierra Leone—where we met with African women to learn about the problems they were facing and to witness some programs that were working well that we could support and replicate in other places.

We visited a papaya farm cooperative where women were given a stake in the profits, and then we had dinner with young women studying at the university while working and taking care of younger siblings and older relatives (and fending off marriage proposals). They were determined to get their tickets punched for independence, security, and opportunity through education.

Our last stop was in Freetown, Sierra Leone—a country whose civil war was just barely behind them. The poverty was much more pronounced than in the other countries we'd visited. Desperation was everywhere.

We went to a women's hospital that focused on maternal health and saving young babies (Sierra Leone has one of the highest maternal and infant mortality rates in the world). The few doctors available to the hospital worked nonstop, trying to ensure healthy births for mothers and children. There wasn't enough of anything—beds, instruments, nurses, supplies. They did the most they could with what little was available.

During that visit, I was hoping to ask a nurse for some cream for a bite I'd gotten on the inside of my forearm in the middle of the night. (I was alone—Peter was back in the States!) It itched like crazy and was getting bigger and redder with every hour. (Spider? Monster mosquito? I cringed as I pictured what bit me…and how long it was there while I dozed. The thing must've been the size of a small bird.)

Just as I was about to approach one of the nurses, our guide announced that we were going to visit the unit for malnourished children.

Forget the bite.

There were eight children in the ward. I had never seen children so tiny, so emaciated, except on television during famine coverage or on commercials for charitable appeals. That was nothing like seeing them in person, making eye contact, and smelling their little baby bodies in the heat.

I particularly remember one little boy. He looked about the age of my friend's toddler back home. I asked a nurse about him. He wasn't a toddler. He was seven years old. That crushed me. She asked if I'd like to hold him.

"He craves human contact," she said.

I sat on his cot with him in my arms and sang him the nursery rhymes I could remember and told him about my dog back in the States. He gripped my finger as tightly as his weak hand could. He felt as tiny as a bird. It was very difficult to hand him back to the nurse.

"I think he'll be okay," she said, perhaps more for my comfort than anything. I prayed she was right.

As we finished up at the hospital with the chief administrator, we asked him lots of questions: "Do you have enough formula, vitamins? What do you need most of all? How can we help? What can we do?"

"Just please don't forget us," he said.

We would never forget them. We promised.

Next, already emotionally wrecked, we went to a place that opened and broke my heart and also, over time, led me to another mentor and role model. It was the Aberdeen Women's Centre, also in Freetown. The small medical hospital was founded by Dame Ann Gloag. Ann is Scottish and worked as a nurse in a burn unit for years before she and her brothers started Stagecoach, a bus company. They were extremely successful over time and grew their business worldwide.

As the company expanded, Ann took the Africa accounts. As soon as she got there and saw the conditions for maternal health care, she said, "This will never do." A loving mother herself, she took on the problems by establishing many charities that got really good results. She refused to pay bribes. In return, she earned respect.

I didn't meet Ann until a year later. I'd been asked to moderate a conversation between President Bush and the First Lady at a fundraiser for Mercy Ships. Mercy Ships is a surgical floating hospital that serves along the west coast of Africa. Ann was on the nonprofit's board.

I was asked at my table what had inspired my interest in Africa. I explained that my trip with the Bushes in 2008 lit the initial spark but that my trip with the ONE Campaign had solidified a lifelong devotion in me. I told them about a "Scottish heiress" that started a vaginal fistula clinic and how I'd witnessed the pain and suffering of women and girls who do not have access to quality maternal health care and how seeing them learn how to count for the first time nearly brought me to my knees.

My dinner partners said, "Oh—she's not an heiress. She's a businesswoman. And she's sitting right behind you."

Believe it or not, Ann is even smaller than me—she's tiny and mighty. Her eyes are a bright and deep blue, and she smiles easily. We hit it off immediately.

I asked her all about the clinic that I'd visited. I learned more about how she had hired drivers to take her to villages deep in the bush so that she could convince tribal leaders to allow her to take women with fistulas to the city where they would be surgically repaired.

She forged some good relationships and delivered on her promise. She takes the women to the clinic and allows them to rest for one week. The next week they have the surgery and recover. After that, she gives them another week of rest, relaxation, and education. They learn a skill, like how to make curtains, so they can earn some money.

One of Ann's rules is that the patients do not have to do any work while they're there. No cooking or cleaning. For them, it's the first time in their lives that they can just relax and put their feet up.

Most of those women would have, on average, ten pregnancies in their lives and half of their babies would not survive past the age of five.

In recent years, Ann's team has introduced "SunnyMoney" solar charging stations, which have given the women so much clout and power when they return to their villages. Cell phones are as ubiquitous in Africa as the United States. And what does everyone with a cell phone need? A way to charge it. In Africa, that's often a problem. Electricity and outlets aren't plentiful. So, imagine returning to your family and friends, renewed in health and with a solar charger as well, able to make money and take care of yourself. Now, that's power!

To spread the word about their work, Ann and her team helped with a documentary called *Shout Gladi Gladi*, which you can see at www.shoutgladigladi.com. You can also learn more about her work at www.freedomfromfistula.org.

Inspired by our evening with Mercy Ships, a year later Peter and I went to Congo and stayed on the *Africa Mercy*. We put together a package for Fox News—with Peter working the video camera like a pro from the front lines of journalism—which aired on *The Five* when we got back. We've become active supporters of Mercy Ships. We saw how the volunteers spread hope and healing to the world's forgotten poor. And they did it without wasting a penny—I've never seen a dollar stretched so far.

In 2019, Ann became Dame Ann Gloag, recognized by Queen Elizabeth II for her considerable charitable work. Peter and I flew to Scotland for a party in Ann's honor to celebrate her achievements so far. In the elevator at the hotel, a little girl I'd learn was Ann's great-granddaughter said in a heavy Scottish accent, "I got to meet Olly Murs!" And I said, "Oh, that's very neat," embarrassed by how my American accent must sound to her (colonial roots die hard). I later learned that Olly Murs is like the Nick Jonas of England. She was right—he's pretty cool and put on a great show as we danced in "Scottish cocktail attire" (which I later found out meant very nice dresses for women and kilts worn in the *traditional* style or tartan trousers with tuxedo jackets for men—we didn't embarrass ourselves... on that front, at least). It was a fine time, a party fit for a dame.

I tell you about Ann because I think it's important to keep finding women that inspire you like she did for me. She makes me want to keep pushing, trying, and creating. Ann didn't let "no" stop her from doing something that was good and right.

She took on an awesome responsibility. Look at what one woman can do for others.

That's why I consider Dame Ann one of my role models today. I admire how she lives her faith—to whom much is given, much is required. She also lives by a strict ethical code, refusing to pay bribes that are so common in Africa but that hurt the people while padding the pockets of the powerful. And Ann does the work of twenty people—her skills are impressive, but so is how she lives her life. She's had setbacks and heartaches, pushed through them, and has a living legacy that she knows will continue to grow. Imagine making an impact like that.

I, too, try to live with gratitude and to push for better by paying it forward, especially when it comes to mentoring. I feel that's my calling right now.

And it is gratifying to do so here in America where being an educated American woman means you're already so far ahead in life. You have a head start that most women around the globe could never imagine.

So: What will *you* do?

It's exciting to imagine.

FINDING A MENTOR

Be on the lookout for good mentors. Sometimes you'll have formal relationships with a mentor, possibly set up by your company to help foster good training for young professionals.

But more often than not, you'll be mentored by people you admire in informal ways. You'll be taken under their wing or get to see them in action at the annual sales meeting. You might even get to work directly for them.

In August 2020, I interviewed Secretary Condi Rice for an event celebrating the hundredth anniversary of women's suffrage. I asked her about mentors that had a big influence on her. Here's what she said:

> I was *really* fortunate to have mentors who advocated for me. One of the mentors was Brent Scowcroft, who was the national security adviser to George H. W. Bush. He took me under his wing as a young assistant professor at Stanford in the early 1980s, and he really helped advocate for my career. We have to remember that no one gets there on their own; there are always mentors that are part of the story.
>
> I would say this to young women: I know it's hard when you see a field you want to excel in, a field where there isn't anybody who looks like you, but if I had been waiting for a black female Soviet specialist role model, I would still be waiting. My role models and mentors were white men, old white men, because that's who dominated my field. Sometimes your role model or mentor may not look like you. George H. W. Bush was a great mentor. Mentors can do a lot to break down barriers around race or gender by just advocating for people they believe in.

As she says, you may find a mentor in unexpected places. I certainly never imagined that I'd get to be mentored by the first black female Soviet specialist who went on to become the first black female secretary of state!

Her advice is good whether you're the mentee or the mentor—advocate for people you believe in.

STOP—WAIT A MINUTE

Before you can do the "big thing," you have to get the basics right. This means making good personal decisions a habit. Being thoughtful about your choices. Embracing the decision making that comes with adulthood.

Instilling personal discipline over your choices is a way to find more freedom. How? Well, if you have a code that you live by, or a goal you're trying to reach, then decisions that would help you keep your code and achieve your goal are easier to make.

For example, maybe you want to reduce your sugar intake, get more rest or more exercise, read more books, or learn a new skill. All those things are good ideas, and you can do all of them—it all depends on you. No one else can do it for you (they've got their own problems to deal with).

Here's my point: whatever problem you're trying to solve, you have the power to try and the will to succeed. You can choose to finally address this problem or you can make excuses. It's up to you. You make the choice.

Now that you've answered the question about what the biggest problem you're trying to tackle is, I have another question: How badly do you want to solve it?

I can push you, pull you, even inspire you. But you have to do the work.

The good news is there's so much you can do that will improve your workday. If you implement the steps in this next chapter, you'll set yourself up to be more resilient and more valuable, building that foundation that helps you make sure everything will be all right.

And while you think about your career and your personal life, consider adding a plan for service to others—it will open your heart and give you that perspective that keeps you grounded and grateful, as well as introduce you to a whole new set of friends.

To recap—how to spot a role model and reach out to them:

1. Make a list of some people you admire and consider role models, and ask friends who they admire.
2. Write down your role model's key characteristics—what of those can you emulate?
3. Read or watch what they do—this is especially important should you ever get the chance to meet them. People respond better if they know you've invested time in their work.
4. Send a note of compliment to their social media—you'll be surprised how many people manage their own accounts. And compliments are much more likely to get a response than trolls!
5. Keep a running list of questions that you'd love to ask them. Imagine that by chance you end up in an elevator with them—what would you want to ask to ensure you use that time wisely?

Now that you've assessed your career and considered your role models, you're ready to dive into some practical advice for improving your work product. Take a deep breath—there's a lot in this next chapter.

~~~~~~

CHAPTER 5

How Can You Improve Your Workday?

Now that we have nailed down your biggest problem and thought about role models that inspire you, it's time to move into suggestions for how to solve it.

My goal in this chapter is to help you improve your day-to-day work product and put you on a steadier and speedier career path. Growing up, I'd hear sayings like "If you want to be a cowgirl, you're going to have to put on more than boots and a hat." You have to work and work at getting better *at* work.

I've broken these tips for success into smaller categories—that way they'll be easier to digest (sort of like tapas).

I want to help you become more reliable and resilient, and more efficient and satisfied in doing a good day's work. If you want to succeed, you need to be the one people can count on—the one they call when they really need something and when they need something handled well.

You're transitioning from your starting position or second job to being the boss and a leader. This is an exciting time for you, but you have to put in some extra work to climb this ladder and set yourself apart from the competition.

It's very important that you start working on self-improvement when you're in your twenties. Investing in yourself in your third decade is essential. Your twenties are not the time to roll the dice on your future, to bop around breezing through life all healthy and young, trusting that everything you want and need will fall into place when you hit thirty. It doesn't work that way.

One of the most important modern books on this is *The Defining Decade: Why Your Twenties Matter—And How to Make the Most of Them Now*, by Dr. Meg Jay. She is a clinical psychologist who focuses her practice on this demographic. In her book she provides case studies of her work with young people who are not taking anything too seriously while believing that everything will fall into place in ten years.

If you put in the work in your twenties, it'll pay off in your thirties and beyond. By all means, enjoy your youth and have some fun, but be smart about it.

And if you're reading this in your thirties or forties, you'll find that there is still room for personal improvement—or you may be in a position where you're managing younger people and you desperately need them to take things a bit more seriously in order to meet the company's goals.

Some of this advice you may have heard before and other bits may seem obvious. Maybe so, but ask yourself this: Are you taking all of it to heart? Are you consistent about applying the right approaches to your work?

For others, this chapter may be overwhelming. Don't worry—all this advice doesn't have to be deployed at once (though it could for you overachievers!). If you need to, break it up into three things you can do a week. The next week, add three more, and so on. Soon, you'll be firing on all cylinders and getting ready to move into the corner office!

Let's begin.

Section #1: It's go time

Harness the power of intention. Consistency gets results; your foundation for success is built upon good habits.

TICKTOCK—MAKING THE CLOCK WORK FOR YOU

When I was a kid and was asked to clean my room, I'd start by making a list of all the things I needed to do, and I'd make it really detailed, like, "Desk—put away papers, straighten books, clean lamp, dust tops, polish wood..." I put more time into making my list than it would have taken just to start cleaning.

I liked making lists because I loved crossing things off. That sense of accomplishment is like a runner's high to me. Give me another gold star on my chart, Mom!

As an adult, I still make lists, but I've learned to pare it down. A long list with everything you could possibly need to do isn't useful.

Instead, I recommend having a daily to-do list of just three to five tasks, rather than a list of twenty-five or more. The reason is that you will realistically only get through about five tasks in any one day. It keeps you more honest, and it stops you from feeling overwhelmed.

If time management is a real challenge for you, I suggest you track how you use your time for a couple of weeks (like tracking calories). You can't fix what you don't measure. What you find may surprise you. Who knew it took that long to figure out what you were going to wear that day or how much time you were wasting scrolling through Twitter? For all of us, there is something we could adjust to make time work better for us. Take control of the clock so that it doesn't control you.

STYLE YOUR WAY TO CONFIDENCE

Keeping up appearances really does matter.

Dress for success is a tried and true tip that has been around for decades. There's a reason for that—it works.

Many companies are now much less formal than they used to be (thank goodness—the item of clothing I hated the most was nylons. They were the worst. I haven't worn them in years, hallelujah!), but there is usually a dress code and there's also common sense.

If you're in the medical field or working in a lab, the dress code is much easier. Uniforms are great in this regard. But if you're in an office environment, or in sales where you're out meeting customers, then having appropriate outfits is a must.

It really shouldn't have to be said, but just to make sure—avoid anything that is too short, low cut, or tight. If those are your most comfortable clothes, think of taking it down a notch from a nine to a seven. You can be you—just be sensible about it.

Employers aren't asking for much here. You don't have to dress like you're going to church, but have clean clothes, ironed if necessary, that you can feel good in during a day's work. And keep your shoes in shipshape condition—polished and in good repair. This makes your shoes last longer, too.

You've heard it before, and it's true: you should dress for the job you want, not the job you have. Why? Well, if you step it up a little bit, make an effort, then you'll set yourself apart, make good first impressions, and conjure up good things when the bosses are talking about who should pitch the new business, go on the site survey, or get a promotion. (I'll never forget when my assistant last year sent me a meme of Glinda the Good Witch in *The Wizard of Oz*—the caption said, "Me dressing for the job I want." Very funny!) Believe me when I tell you that people really do notice these things.

Another good tip is having a "safety suit" in the office for just-in-case situations. Let's say something happens during the day when suddenly you need to be in a meeting with the CEO who is visiting from out of town. The problem is that it's "casual Friday" and you look like you should be hanging out on a roof deck drinking margaritas for lunch.

What are you going to do if you have nothing to change into? I know someone who ended up getting a promotion because of an emergency hearing in a case and the lead lawyer didn't wear a suit that day and didn't have one at the office. My friend did. She raised her hand, changed into her suit, and handled the hearing. She showed that she was ready for a promotion. She was prepared—you should be, too.

By the way, this advice applies to any videoconferencing as well. It's true no one can see you from the top down, so wear jeans or whatever you prefer—but always make sure that you're appropriately dressed and looking sharp for team meetings or client presentations, even if they're only happening through a video screen. There are plenty of examples of "videoconferencing failures"—amirite?

I confess that my preference is jeans in the winter, shorts in the summer. During the "work from home" period in 2020, I'd put on a colorful sweater or business jacket and be wearing khaki shorts and flip-flops for the shows. Semicasual worked for me as long as I was reading the teleprompter from my guest bedroom.

Oh, and as a reminder, only wear your UGGs to travel to and from the office. Never wear them all day *in* the office. They make you shuffle. A while back, I watched for a couple of years as this one young woman would wear her UGGs all day long and she'd shuffle to and from the copier, to and from the kitchen, to and from the restroom. I wanted to yell into the hallway, "Pick up your feet so that it looks like you want to be here!" but instead I just keep putting this advice in my books.

When it comes to fashion, I really need some guidance. I didn't have the best fashion sense when I was growing up. I remember my mom ironing a big yellow *D* on the back pocket of my jeans because I wanted a design on the pocket (Jordache, Mom, Jordache). And she would sew an Izod Lacoste alligator onto my button-downs instead of paying for a real one. I think that one blue gator ended up on three different shirts over the years. So, I'm a little scarred.

There are professionals who can help. I've met a wonderful stylist in New York City named Karen Kleber. Karen knows what it's like to be starting out and not knowing what to wear to work. When you're up to your eyeballs in student loans, your rent is due, and you don't know what to wear for your big presentation, nothing in your closet seems right. You feel awkward and out of place. You don't know where to begin to dress the part.

I asked her for her top tips to get you on a smart path to achieve your executive presence:

1. Think and dress professionally

Identify a style mentor in your industry. Observe and talk to her. Emulate her style. Then make it your own.

But don't go overboard. Tone it down. You are not the focus—you are part of the *team*.

If you're dressed to go out for the evening, you are not in the right outfit.

And no towering heels until you're the CEO!

2. Get ready for business

Your work wardrobe is harmonious in color and style. It suits your body type and fits properly.

As you learn about your industry, understand the dress code and follow your style mentor's lead.

No more frivolous buying. Establish a color palette so pieces work flawlessly with each other.

Buy less; wear more. Rinse and repeat!

3. Do your research

You don't need $$$ to dress professionally.

Learn about fabrics and quality, then shop pre-owned or off-brand, trade with friends, or delve into the online wardrobe rental sites, like Rent the Runway.

Take pictures of your choices in the dressing room to see yourself objectively.

Then reevaluate before purchasing. (I needed this advice, too!)

4. Be prepared; you never know!

You are representing not only yourself but also the company that hired you—as well as your aspirations.

Challenging days can bring you down, but keep looking up. Dress the part. Feel your confidence.

Project the self-assured woman that you are, and you'll be on your way.

STAND UP STRAIGHT

Allow me to share my obsession with posture. Not your posture, mine.

I'm a short person. I stand at five feet even, and that's on a good day, when I am standing up straight and feeling good. With gravity and age, however, I would bet I am clocking in a bit under that height. There's nothing I can do about how tall I am, but there is a lot I can do to appear taller.

Think back to when you were a kid. You probably got admonished once in a while from your parents, teachers, or coaches to stand up straighter. Why? Because people who have good posture appear more confident, positive, and assured. Bad posture can send the wrong signal—that you're tired, weary, and not interested. People that cared about you as a kid wanted you to get into a habit of standing up tall in order to project confidence.

As adults, we see over and over how people that have good posture are more likely to be tapped for special projects and promoted more quickly than others. Your energy precedes you—before you even introduce yourself or look someone in the eye, people can feel what energy you're giving off. A closed posture is negative. An open posture is positive. Look around; study people. You'll see this is true—in sports, athletes utilize good posture to show their opponent they're confident. Watch how tennis professionals walk onto the court before a big match. Or boxers, facing each other before the first bell rings. They stand up straight with their shoulders back and their chins up—confident and fearless. That's a lot more intimidating than someone scrunched over, looking timid and insecure.

Unfortunately, our modern lifestyle isn't helping our posture—it is working against it. We spend so much time hunched over on our phones, laptops, and books that we are rounded and closed because our shoulders are pulled forward and our head is pulling our neck down.

Over time, all of this can lead to chronic pain and extreme discomfort. I got into some bad habits when I was waitressing in college—I would carry a huge tray of food or drinks with my right arm. And to this day when I put my arm in that position, I have an ache around my shoulder blade.

When I went from waitressing to working in offices, I developed bad habits. I tapped furiously on my BlackBerry (that's an old-school iPhone) and held the phone between my ear and my shoulder, causing a pinch in my neck. I also carried a heavy tote bag on my right shoulder, which pulled me down on one side and caused my hips to get out of alignment.

To help alleviate the pain, I took a lot of over-the-counter pain relief. I even got a prescription for a muscle relaxant. I started seeing chiropractors (not everyone's cup of tea, but it worked for me), and I spent a fortune on massages. I had Peter rub Bengay on my back, joking that it was my new perfume but cringing when I sat next to someone on an airplane because the smell is unmistakable. All of that would help me feel better for a day or so, but then I'd be right back into the pain. And this is well before I was forty!

Then I wrote *And the Good News Is…* and my posture completely fell apart. I spent so many hours typing, editing, and revising that by the time it was finished, I was a wreck. I could see in the mirror that I was rounded forward. I didn't like how it looked. I really didn't like how I felt. I was in a lot of pain most of the time.

As I was walking in Central Park one day, all stooped, I realized that I had to do something about it. I had to make better choices and invest in my health.

Over the next several years, I worked at my posture nearly every day. But I will tell you it hasn't been easy. I have to constantly think about it, reminding myself that if I hold myself correctly, I won't get that pain in my back. I started wearing a posture loop when I traveled on planes and trains—and far from looking at me like I was crazy, most of my seatmates asked me where they could get one. I still take three Pilates classes a week, and in addition to other exercise, I am committed to doing at least one additional exercise for my posture a day. Most evenings, after *The Five*, I spend ten to fifteen minutes following a video on YouTube (Yoginimelbourne), PilatesBarreOnDemand with Tracey Mallett, or a video on my Peloton app.

One of my concerns about writing this book was what might happen to my posture if I spent all that additional time on my laptop. So I designed a way, with one of my Pilates instructors, to keep myself correctly aligned. I lean back against two or three firm pillows with my head supported. I have another pillow or blanket on my lap and set my computer on top of that so that I don't have to look down and strain my neck. It probably looks ridiculous, but I have invested too much into getting my posture into a better place for me.

I know that I'm practically begging you to address your posture early in your working life. But trust me—it's harder to correct it the longer you put if off.

Plus, it just might be what helps you stand head and thrown-back shoulders above the competition for a new job or a promotion.

Section #2: The power of attitude

You control your own destiny

BE RELENTLESSLY PUNCTUAL

I'm the kind of person that's rarely late. I learned this from an early age. My parents were early risers, and on the ranch in the summers, we woke with the sun and just about went to sleep when the sun went down. It was a natural cycle. And as my grandfather (and probably yours) would say, "If you're not early, you're late."

Most of my "work nightmares" have always had to do with being late—the stress, even in my sleep, is unbearable. I remember once I dreamed that I was at the White House, but that I couldn't find the briefing room, and then I realized I was wearing jeans and I was going to have to find another outfit to wear but I was already late and, well, thankfully I woke up and realized I had beaten my alarm clock once again. I've had dreams like that about Fox News as well—that I am walking to work but I misjudged the time and I am going to be late, have not been to hair and makeup, and I'm going to have to call the boss and tell them I screwed up. (I've also had several nightmares involving Greg Gutfeld, but who doesn't? Ha!)

Scary dreams aside, working in television suits me fine. When we're live at 5:00 p.m., I can't ever be a casual five minutes late and neither can anyone else. In over ten years of working at Fox News, I've never known any of our folks not to be ready (even though we sometimes cut it close and give our audio techs and stage managers minor heart attacks—sorry about that, Allison!).

I also worked for a president who was always early. If we had a policy meeting in the Oval Office scheduled for 2:00 p.m., you'd better be ready to start at 1:45 p.m. Often he wanted to start even earlier than that. Once, I went to lunch with former press secretary George Stephanopoulos. We were near the White House and had just ordered our meals when I got an email that said the president was ready to start a meeting. He was forty-five minutes early. I turned red and looked up at George to apologize. "Go," he said. "No one understands more than I do." And while we never made up for that lunch, I'll never forget his understanding of the situation.

Sometimes President Bush was running so early that we had to make up reasons to stall him. For example, he would be champing at the bit to start a press conference, and I'd have to hold him back with some distraction until I was sure the reporters had found their seats. I kept a little bit of media gossip in my back pocket for just those occasions. He loved to hear what was going on behind the scenes with the White House press corps. (There should probably be a press corps for the White House press corps.)

Suffice to say, having to be on time works for me. I enjoy the challenge of being punctual. It is a little bit like a competition with yourself. Beat the clock!

I thrive in an environment that is deadline driven. Now, you might not. You might struggle with getting to work on time, or you might lose yourself in a project that makes you a few minutes late to a meeting or a conference call.

I believe everyone should get about ten passes for being late in their professional life. Things happen, of course. But remember, punctuality is a sign of respect.

If anyone has to wait for you to get a meeting started, they get irritated. Some might even feel disrespected, especially if there's no good reason you're late or if it happens regularly. There's really nothing good about showing up to a meeting late and having to say, "Excuse me," while you find a seat, all eyes on you wondering just what was so important that you couldn't be there on time. Not to mention perhaps missing some important information. And trust me—the boss is keeping count.

A few simple fixes:

- Commit to being on time. Make it a goal that you will be on time to everything, even your yoga class, for an entire month. This includes meeting your friends for brunch—don't leave people hanging. You'll gain respect for being courteous and it will alleviate unnecessary stress. You may find that you have more time to spend on things you love doing if you make being punctual a habit.
- Try to be fifteen minutes early. That way, even if you miss that, you're still not late. Trick yourself into being on time.
- Go through your calendar and see if you can find ways to help improve your punctuality. Have you put too many meetings too close together? Are you always late to the 8:30 a.m. meeting—if so, why? What can you do to change things? If you need to get up earlier, start slowly, in ten-minute chunks, and gradually build up to half an hour. Or—and this is a novel

idea—go to bed earlier. As I said, I'm an early-to-bed kind of person, but I'm always well rested and ready to go and I can wake up before my alarm and not be miserable. Developing this habit means that you may miss some parties, but I promise that that's not the end of the world. There will be lots of fun nights; maybe Saturday night is your night to go big or go home—that just means that Sunday night you pass on the late dinner and get to bed early. You can train yourself to be more of a morning person, even if you have to fake it for a while.

Being late means that no matter how talented you are, you don't come across as committed and serious. Being punctual shows you care, you're responsible, and you can be given more duties.

WHAT'S LUCK GOT TO DO WITH IT? RESPECT ACCOMPLISHMENTS.

When you're new to working full-time for a company, it takes a while to get used to being the low person on the totem pole. And while you know that, over the years, you're going to climb up to the top, it can sometimes be discouraging or disappointing when you're not invited to certain meetings, fancy dinners, or big events at neat places that you've always wanted to go to.

Even so, at all times resist the urge to tell your boss, "You're so lucky!" even if you're genuinely excited for them. You'll hear this phrase a lot over the years: "Luck is when preparation meets opportunity." It's funny—I thought my dad came up with that, because it's something dads say; however, it turns out, the quote is attributed to a Roman philosopher named Seneca. He knew this way back in the first century CE. But I bet he heard it from his dad, too.

Here's what Seneca and our dads are trying to say: hard work pays off over time. You have to learn the difference between luck and earning something. Luck is a game of chance, like winning the lotto or playing craps at a casino, while merit is something you earn over time. It's when your efforts start to turn into, "Hey, could you join us for the meeting with the clients that are flying in from London? We'd like you to present on the new campaign." And suddenly it hits you. Aha! The harder you work, the "luckier" you seem to get. As Louis Pasteur put it, "Luck favors the prepared mind."

And even if you still think your boss is lucky, just don't say it. Instead, ask her if there's anything you can do to make sure she has what she needs to make the event a success. Offer to make a packet of information about the hosts or the table guests so that she can get familiar with them before she arrives. When the event is over, ask your boss what the most memorable moment was, or who she was most interested in following up with after the dinner. There are ways for you to participate even if you aren't there. And don't worry—you'll be invited soon enough.

PERSPECTIVE WITH A CAPITAL P

In the White House press office, I had an assistant press secretary in charge of handling all the personnel announcements for the president's nominations for appointments (to the cabinet, boards and commissions, and ambassadorships). I trusted her and the personnel office to manage all of that. I would do a quick final sign-off, but otherwise I didn't get too involved.

Well, Christmas Eve, when we were all ready for a break for the holiday, my staffer got a call from a journalist at the *Los Angeles Times* asking about a board of supervisors appointment the president had announced for Radio and TV Martí, which is part of the US broadcasting efforts in Cuba.

The reporter asked if my office could confirm the nomination had been made. Yes, it had. And did we know that one of the people we appointed had been dead for eleven years? (Not *always* a deal breaker in government employment, admittedly.) Ummmm... "Let me call you back," she said. She came to see me, blushing and trying to hold it together. She worried that I would be angry. I wasn't—I just said, "Let's try to see what this is all about."

For a few hours, we scrambled. There wasn't a good explanation from the personnel office. My staffer was asked six times by the reporter how we could possibly have nominated a dead person.

"What are we supposed to do? Check the obituaries every day?!" a manager in the personnel office said. (Tip: this is not a helpful response.)

She ended up with a less-than-satisfying quote for the story along the lines of, "All we know is the president very much cares for the people of Cuba."

Ugh! That's one of those quotes that you play over and over in your mind for years. Talk about not funny at the time but something we laugh about now.

Writing that reminds me of another one. This one still gives me a burning feeling in my stomach when I remember it. We were at the G8 meeting in Kyoto, Japan. The weather was horrible. A dense fog had settled over the mountain, and for three days we couldn't see a thing. It was like white butcher-block paper had been taped to all the windows. It was a busy time—so much happening with the wars in Iraq and Afghanistan, a worrying economic downturn approaching, and a presidential election underway in which both candidates were using George W. Bush as their punching bag. We were battling with reporters all day, every day.

In preparation for foreign trips, the National Security Council would provide a read-ahead book for the press corps that contained a lot of great research and information about the leaders the president would meet with and the agenda items. One of the NSC staff members had been out on sick leave for quite a while but had returned to work just before the trip and insisted she had the capacity to do the books. We were grateful for the help.

Except. When we got to Japan, it was pointed out to us that instead of the Italian prime minister's official biography being in the briefing book, we had just put in the Wikipedia page for Silvio Berlusconi. Now, Berlusconi is a man with a colorful life, shall we say. (I'll let you google it. PS: NSFW.) And the official US government briefing book included this line in his bio: "Loved by some, but hated by many, Prime Minister Berlusconi..."

Well, this was not good. One member of the senior staff was particularly furious and wanted answers. I took full responsibility and thought of how I could fix it (I hadn't read the entire briefing book—it never occurred to me to check the bios of the leaders). I dreaded the day.

That evening, after handling other crises like a whack-a-mole pro, it was time for the leaders to gather for a photo before the dinner. I was in the room when Berlusconi walked in. He looked around the room. We made eye contact. I've never fainted, but I imagined falling over at this moment.

Berlusconi made a beeline to me, his arms opened wide, and said, loudly enough for everyone to hear, "Dana, Dana, Dana— don't worry about it! Besides...it's true!" and he wrapped me in a bear hug. (He's an Italian—we hug. It was all good.)

I was so grateful for his reaction, how he chose to handle it. He could've gotten mad, and maybe he had at first. But he kept everything in perspective and decided it was something to laugh about, not dwell over. I will always remember that example of kindness and leadership. Bunga bunga! (As I said, look it up.)

Everyone is going to have problems to deal with every day. Some will be bigger than others. Keeping them in perspective is key. Make a checklist of how to handle a problem, keep it handy, and refer to it when needed. Some possible considerations: Get all the information before losing your cool. Learn to exercise good judgment on whether and when to alert your boss to a problem. Ask yourself, How important is this? Is it a matter that requires interrupting a meeting? Or can it wait until there's a quieter moment in the day to bring it to her attention? You'll get the hang of this—inevitably, at some point a boss will ask why you didn't bring a matter to them sooner. And at another point you'll be told that something isn't a priority right now and it'll have to wait. Timing is important—calibrate your communications to fit the situation and the mood. This will demonstrate that you know how to assess what's critical, what's important, and what's just trivial (though sometimes the trivial is good for a light moment!).

When you're not sure what to do, take a deep breath. Assess. And remember—a lot of problems that seemed like the biggest screwups are things that you end up laughing about years later. I have more than my fair share of these.

Learn to laugh about them and at yourself. It's better than crying yourself to sleep wrapped around a bottle of cabernet. And remember: none of this will matter in the long run. Or even by next Saturday, most likely.

NO MORE WORRIES

I noticed a trend a while ago that started to really bug me. Since I have very busy days with not a lot of spare time, I have to be smart about how I fill any of the extra time I have. I'm blessed with a lot of requests—for me to give a speech, host a charity fundraiser, mentor a young person, attend a conference, etc. Because of my schedule, I have to say no to most opportunities, especially as they happen outside of New York City and I'd have to take a day off to get there. I can't exactly work from home or on the road, given the daily shows that I do in Manhattan.

Anyway, the point is that when you ask me, for example, if I can attend a meeting, give a speech, or go to lunch (I haven't gone to lunch in three years!), and I say, "I am unable to attend, but thank you for the invitation," please don't say, "No worries."

Why does this bother me? Maybe it's because I haven't gone to lunch in three years. But more likely, it's because I already have enough to worry about. My not being able to come to your event shouldn't be on my list of worries.

I suggest saying from the start, "I realize your schedule is very busy and your time is limited, but we'd like to propose [insert request here]."

And if I can't do it, to respond by saying, "I appreciate the response. We would love to have you at some point, and if there's ever a way to make it happen when it would work with your schedule, we'd be thrilled to have you."

That would make me want to take your call or answer your email the next time.

"No worries" sounds like I'm the one that should feel bad, and I really don't need any more to worry about.

And try to respect people who are using their good judgment to say no to too many requests. You'll be in that same position one day soon.

Section #3: Commit to excellence

Start with a dream, set your goals, and relentlessly try to reach them

HAVE RÉSUMÉ, WILL TRAVEL

I'm a believer in being at the right place at the right time, which means having your eyes and ears open at all times for opportunities.

As I mentioned in chapter 2, I got my first job as a press secretary on Capitol Hill because of a chance meeting at a hockey game.

(Go Avs!) Thankfully, I had just arrived in Washington DC and had an updated résumé ready to send.

However, that's not usually what I experience with people— their résumés are not up-to-date. That means that your current role, accomplishments, responsibilities, and skills are not readily available to send at a moment's notice. And it takes a while to put together a good résumé that won't just be shuffled to the bottom of the pile.

Since timing is everything, be prepared with an updated résumé or a one-sheet biography that you can get to someone at a moment's notice. I recommend updating it once every three to four months—review, refine, enhance, and cut so that if someone brings up a job that you would love to apply for, you're ready to go. This also can come in handy for annual reviews, salary negotiations, or promotion opportunities.

Here's what I look for in a résumé: solid presentation of duties and skills, progression from first job to current position, a little life, a little sparkle. I cringe at industry or résumé jargon. I prefer résumés that are one page, but if merited, a second page is fine. If you've moved around a lot or have had a lot of jobs in a short period of time, try to explain why. I see upward mobility as a plus and am not too concerned about longevity at companies if you've been promoted and moved up the ladder. And if there's a fun experience or unique hobby (great at oyster shucking), include it. I love to see people who are adventurous (taught English in Vietnam), ran a marathon, took chances, or did something special (volunteered at a bird sanctuary)— whatever will help make you stand out, use it to your advantage.

What can you include that would catch my eye? (A picture of your dog? Maybe!)

JOB-HOPPING AND EXITING GRACEFULLY

You may have heard tales of how someone spent forty-five years with a company, and that may sound absolutely crazy to you. Nearly gone are the days when someone would stay with one company for their entire career. The job market is much more dynamic than it used to be, and people are very much on the move.

In the early part of your career, you'll be itching to move up. Entry-level jobs are meant to be that—entry. You build skills from there—your foundation. In my experience, most young women learn quickly and are ready for their next job right way.

Does it "look bad" if you move around too much? Well, if you have a new job with a different company every six months, then I'd be wary about hiring you. Changing jobs as often as you change your Instagram profile pic is not a sign of stability.

However, if you demonstrate that you've spent a reasonable amount of time learning a job and have moved up, showing progression and growth, then I'd see that as a good thing. It indicates you're hungry for more, ambitious, and that if you come on board with me, then I better be able to provide you challenging opportunities and show you there's a plan for advancement.

Before you can start a great new job, you have to resign from your current job. Doing so gracefully is very important. You do not want to burn bridges. The people you worked for will always be a possible reference check for the rest of your career. What do you want them to say about you? That you were a wonderful employee with a bright future and they were sad to see you go but realized you had a great opportunity and didn't want to hold you back? Or that you were unreliable, unappreciative, and uncooperative—and that you went to lunch one day and never came back? (This actually happened to a friend of mine who runs a small business. Her employee sent a text saying, "I quit." Okay, that's her choice—but she burned a bridge and there's no way to rebuild it.)

My advice on leaving a job:

Understand that people naturally think about themselves first. So, when you build up the courage to ask for a quick word with your boss to tell them you're moving on, don't be surprised if their first reaction is, "But how am I going to get your work done?" True, that isn't your problem. And yes, it'd be great if they popped a bottle of champagne to toast to your news, but that isn't realistic.

You can soften the blow by offering to help find and train a replacement (though don't say you won't leave until a new person is hired... that could drag on too long). If there's someone in the organization that you think is ready to take on your role, suggest them. Your recommendation will be welcome. Plus, it's good career karma.

Write a handwritten thank-you note to the supervisor for all that you learned and include a specific anecdote to show you mean it.

Make sure that all your work is done and that the handoff is smooth. You don't want them looking at your desk thinking, "What a mess!"

And follow all the company rules for managing information about the company; for example, do not download files or company IP (intellectual property) that you will then use later in your next job (a friend had a colleague do this and they both ended up in court, nearly bankrupted by the ordeal).

Finally, once you're ready to leave a job, you just really want to get the heck out of there and move on to your next big thing. It could be tempting to vent about your boss or the business environment—but try to save that for a private cocktail hour with friends who don't work there. If you don't have something nice to say, don't say anything at all.

And when you take that final step out the door, hold your head high and appreciate what you learned there (even if it was that you don't want to be like your boss—that's valuable, too). Your next step is to a new opportunity. Crush it.

SAY YES—THEN FOLLOW THROUGH

Any step change in your career is going to come after you've proven you can handle a task, a management challenge, a troublesome client, or a difficult assignment. Instead of being scared of all the "firsts," try to do what my college speech coach suggested: "It's okay to have butterflies in your stomach, as long as you make them fly in formation."

And if that doesn't work, follow the advice of former secretary of education Margaret Spellings, who called me on the morning of my first White House press briefing. I told her I was nervous. She said, "Well, put your big-girl panties on and deal with it."

First-time nerves are normal. Not letting them get the best of you is the challenge.

And you'll make some mistakes—or prove that you're just learning along the way. That's okay!

This happened to me more times than I can count in my career: during my first interviews, while working at PBS in Pueblo, Colorado, and at CBS in Springfield, Illinois, and especially when I switched gears to being a spokesperson instead of a journalist.

The first time I did a call with a reporter as a House press secretary on Capitol Hill, I had no idea what he was talking about. It was so complicated, having to do with the Federal Energy Regulatory Commission, but he kept saying FERC, the acronym, and I actually had to ask him to spell it out for me (FERC became another *f* word for me).

A few years after that, my colleague and dear friend Jeanie Mamo and I were working in August 2005, while many people were on vacation. We were juggling several big stories at once, including the following:

- The Senate confirmation process for John Roberts to the US Supreme Court was underway.
- A grieving mother of a fallen soldier had started a movement against the Iraq War. She was standing at the president's ranch gate wanting to meet. (They had met previously, and another meeting wasn't granted. I've long wondered what would have

happened if we'd just said, "Yes, please come in—let's talk." I think that would have been the better course.)

- The EPA was announcing controversial actions on air quality.
- The Valerie Plame leak investigation was coming to a head.

And those are just the issues I remember off the top of my head.

On those days, I sometimes had to take things just one hour at a time—looking ahead to the entire day was too daunting.

Jeanie and I joked about making "I survived August 2005 at the White House" T-shirts.

Then on Monday, August 29, Hurricane Katrina hit the Gulf Coast. Overnight, the levies broke in New Orleans and we were tested to try to make things right for the victims of the historic storm.

Five days later, the chief justice of the Supreme Court, William Rehnquist, died. My phone rang at nearly midnight—I had been sleeping for about an hour. I picked up my phone and saw it was Peter Baker, who was then with the *Washington Post*. I had to answer.

"Hello?" I said in a sleepy "don't you feel sorry for me?" voice.

"Hi, Dana. I'm sorry to wake you. But we need a statement," he said.

"About what?" I asked.

"Chief Justice Rehnquist just died."

"Oh, what the f*ck next?" I muttered. *That* woke me up. "Oh my goodness, Peter. I didn't mean to say that—can that be off the record?"

I prayed for a bit of mercy.

"Absolutely, of course," he said.

"Thank you," I said, relieved. I'm pretty sure President Bush would *not* have been happy with me if that were on the front page of the *Washington Post*.

Looking back on that hot and muggy month in 2005, I think that's when I found the clutch and the gear to perform at a higher level, to take on a higher level of responsibility, to trust my judgment, and to explain my position clearly and persuasively to senior staff. I also started to feel a lot more comfortable with speaking on behalf of the president. Going through that very tough time working at least eighteen hours a day for over forty-five days was a crucible process of rising from my midlevel staffer career to my role as a principal. Without that trial, I never would have proven to the chief of staff and the president—let alone to myself—that I was ready for more. I had taken on the challenge, gotten through the difficult days, and was stronger for it.

There are other moments that stick out, times when I pushed through—like when I first briefed the president and thought he could probably see me trembling. Or when I first stepped to the podium at the White House and looked out at the reporters—could they tell my legs were shaking?

Then there were firsts in television on Fox News: appearing as a political analyst on *America's Newsroom*, joining the Great American Panel on Sean Hannity's show, and filling in for one of the *Fox & Friends* co-hosts. Of course, the most nervous I'd ever been on TV was the first day as a co-host of *The Five* (even though we believed at the time it was only a temporary, five-week show...it's been going strong since 2011). And yet that was nothing compared to my nerves the first day anchoring my own news show, *The Daily Briefing with Dana Perino*.

For as nervous as they make us, firsts are so important. Every single first gives you an opportunity to show you can do it. Don't shy away from them. Raise your hand, even if you're not confident you can do it. Chances are, you can. And you will. And you'll see that getting uncomfortable is part of making sure everything is okay. Frankly, if you're not uncomfortable every now and then, you're not growing.

Firsts come in all sorts of ways. Presenting a new marketing strategy to a skeptical C-suite audience, standing next to a surgeon as he prepares to use your company's new device and being ready to answer questions while a patient is under the knife (this is what

Peter does for a living—he has a much stronger stomach than mine), or cold-calling a potential new customer. All those things—even though I'm not doing them—give me a little flurry of worry. I'm even nervous for you!

Besides, sometimes you really are the best person for the job, even though you may not realize it yet.

I had a great mentor explain this to me once.

On his last day as White House press secretary, the late Tony Snow knew he needed to shore up my confidence in taking over for him. Tony was universally loved, a wonderful man, and a terrific briefer. The press loved asking him questions, and he loved sparring with them with a little bit of humor to smooth the edges.

Late in the afternoon, Tony came into my office and asked me how I was doing. I admitted I didn't feel very confident about my ability to fill his shoes. He asked me to stand up and walk over to him. He put his hands on my shoulders, and I had to look way up to meet his gaze.

He said, giving me a little shake, "You are better at this than you think you are."

I was modest and demurred. I didn't believe him.

But he persisted until I said, "Okay."

A couple of weeks later, I finished all my briefing books and I'd finally set my copious notes aside and just spoke freely, using my knowledge from all the studying I'd done. I didn't try to brief like Tony did; I just decided to do it my way—mostly because I was short on time to prepare that day.

Well, as with most things when you finally let go and trust yourself, I felt so much better about how it went that day.

And I realized, *Oh, this is what Tony meant. I don't have to be just like him. I can just be myself.*

Recognizing that you have the potential, that you have been preparing for these moments, and that you can deliver results in your own way is empowering—and it can lead to additional professional opportunities and success.

And, of course, more responsibility. (Sorry, you're the one who picked up this book!)

This reminds me of a young woman I mentor. She works in cybersecurity. That's a highly sought-after skill set, and though she's very young and not long out of college, she landed a great new job at a big organization.

About two weeks into it, there was a crisis at her company regarding a cyber vulnerability. She was just learning everyone's names and roles, but the senior staff looked to her to fix the situation. She felt overwhelmed and didn't think she had enough experience to handle the problem. She thought she was being set up for failure.

(I want everyone to put this out of their mind because I hear it often—your bosses are not going to set you up for failure, because if you fail, it will look bad on them. Now, your higher-ups may not give you enough resources and expect too much, and it's your responsibility to manage their expectations, but do not allow yourself to be paranoid and think that someone wants you to fail. That's illogical and unhelpful to you and your organization.)

Anyway, back to the story of my friend. I asked her if she felt she had the right approach to handling the problem. She did. Did she feel like if they didn't do what she suggested, it could result in losses to the company and permanent damage to the clients? Yes. Then I said, "You have to take a deep breath and lead them through it. Show them that you deserve their respect. Damn the torpedoes!" (Or terabytes, I guess, in this instance.)

In the end, the crisis took about a week to manage. When it was successfully completed, her employers had newfound respect for her. Then they gave her twenty other things to fix (the consequences of success!). Embrace it.

Sometimes you're just thrown into the lion's den. Another young woman I've known for years was working for a company that was flying high but suddenly came crashing down as the founder turned out to have been full of crap. The business was in big trouble. No one knew if it would survive.

My friend was in public relations, so every other department would come to her for advice. One day she learned that hundreds of employees were going to be laid off. She was there for the discussion and she felt terrible for her colleagues who were about to lose their jobs. What she didn't anticipate is that the new management would push her to the front of the line—she would have to break the news to them.

Me?! she thought. *Why me? I'm not skilled in this. I don't know what I'm doing. I've never done this before!*

But she didn't voice her doubts out loud. She pulled it together and got through it without crying in front of them, though she understandably lost it in the privacy of her office. Breaking really bad news to people you care about is excruciating.

Something interesting happened to her after that, though. First, she got several messages from the people just laid off, thanking her for how she handled it with such delicacy and compassion. So she kept all of them as trusted people in her network. Second, she got the attention of the new managers that were brought in to turn the company around. Soon after, she got several promotions and then was running the department altogether.

By stepping up to a very uncomfortable challenge, and by rising to the occasion to handle it so well, she made a very good impression. And that's what helped vault her to the top job.

The lesson here: you're capable of more than you think you are, and you're better at it than you think you are. Every time you push yourself, you'll see rewards. And that's how you help ensure you're progressing.

ABL: ALWAYS BE LEARNING

What a time to be alive. There has never been more information—on all subjects—available to us than now. Sometimes it feels like *too much* information, but you can sift through it all and find ways to learn, to be entertained, and to help you network with other people.

One of my favorite ways to add more learning to my schedule is to listen to podcasts. I'm an avid listener. I play podcasts while I get ready in the morning and while I walk to work. Peter and I have a couple that we listen to together when we drive to the Jersey Shore on the weekends. It's efficient and entertaining. And I always learn something new.

I have a long list of political shows that I listen to that help me with my work. I have some by comedians that make me laugh, others that expand my knowledge of technology, and some that give me the background as to how some of my favorite country songs came to be.

I'm a bit of a podcast enthusiast. I recently asked my niece if she listened to any, and Peter interrupted, saying, "If you don't, you will by the end of the weekend because she'll beat it into you." Ha—I just want to share!

Here are some of my favorite podcasts I listen to regularly:

Against the Grain, with Josh Kraushaar
The Argument, by the *New York Times*
The Ben Shapiro Show (This is pronounced very fast, all as one word.)
Fox News Rundown
Intelligence Matters, with Mike Morell
The One with Greg Gutfeld (Have you heard of this guy? I think he might have a future.)
Oprah's Master Class

Pastor Rick's Daily Hope
Politics with Amy Walter
Potomac Watch, by the *Wall Street Journal*
The Remnant, by Jonah Goldberg
Secrets of Wealthy Women, by the *Wall Street Journal*
She Said / She Said, with Laura Kaplan
The Sooper Podcast!
Stay Tuned with Preet
The Strategerist
The Trey Gowdy Podcast
This American Life
What the Hell Is Going On?, with Marc Thiessen and Danielle
   Pletka
WorkLife with Adam Grant
Write You a Song, with Tom Mailey

In addition to listening to podcasts, I've started watching a lot more documentaries. I've always liked documentaries—you can learn about all sorts of topics. And they can be great conversation starters. For example, I'm not a rock climber but I loved *Free Solo* and predicted it would win an Oscar. (It did!) I've learned about the dangers of the drug trade in *The Business of Drugs*, and about important historical figures like Ulysses S. Grant, Winston Churchill, and Muhammad Ali. I never think about this time as wasted—it's all adding up to layers of knowledge I can call upon for work, at networking events, or at dinner with friends. It is an important point; to do well *at* work, it helps to be about more than *just* work.

There are also lots of other ways to learn about...anything! Many universities offer some of their classes for free online—including Harvard! (I'm not kidding—https://online-learning.harvard.edu/catalog/free.) Technology has pushed universities to figure out how to bring the classroom to students wherever they are, whatever their circumstances. So, if you want to get a graduate degree in business administration, you can do that from your kitchen table after your workday (while eating gelato straight from the tub—what could be better?). Trust me, no matter the subject, you can find a class at a reasonable price or even for no cost at all online. It's just a click away! Check out this site: www.coursera.org. (It is an incredible compilation of courses... It makes me want to get another degree. In what? I don't know! That's the fun part.)

Use your time wisely. There are so many tools available to you that we didn't have even fifteen years ago. Take advantage of it. Feed your brain nutritious meals, not just junk food (nonsense YouTube "rabbit-holing" or TikTok dance compilations—Addison Rae is doing just fine without your views).

READ EARLY AND OFTEN

When I worked in the White House, I loved going to meetings called "Policy Time." These were hours blocked for the president's senior advisors to come in to brief him on issues and to weigh the decision in front of him. I always learned so much—it was like going to a lecture with the smartest people on the topic, and all I had to do was listen, as there wasn't going to be an exam afterward (except for when I had to brief reporters on it!).

I made it a habit of reading what we called the "Read Ahead" memo that laid out the issue. By investing a few minutes in reviewing the memo the night or morning before the meeting, I understood the basic problem we were trying to solve.

The memos gave me a sense of where various advisors stood on an issue. Sometimes you'd have one office, such as the National Economic Council, really opposed to something that the Domestic Policy Council wanted to do and that the president thought was important. The goal was to give the president the best information so that he could make a decision.

If I didn't read the document beforehand, I'd have no idea what was going on. And I needed to know so that I could read the room. Because whatever the president decided, I'd have to communicate that to the press. If there was an internal dispute, I had to be able to deftly handle if that was leaked to the media. Not that that ever happens...

Today, I still read a ton before my day gets started. I've always tried to be the most well-read person at the meeting, in the briefing room, during a morning call. It gives me confidence and power.

It also means I can spot problems before they arise, identify conflicts, and set myself apart. I'm blessed with an ability to read quickly, and while I don't have a photographic memory, I can pretty much remember most of what I read and know where to find it again if I need to. I print the articles that I want to refer to during a show. (And if I ever suggest printing something, it's worth reading. I don't waste paper—I promise.)

If you need to add more reading relevant to your work, I suggest setting aside thirty minutes in the morning and the evening, and possibly during lunch, to catch up every day. For articles or trade papers you would like to read but that aren't critical to your daily work, start a "weekend reading" folder in your inbox or print them out. I've been doing this since I was on Capitol Hill. That way I don't feel overwhelmed by trying to get through everything I want to read during the day.

On the weekend when there's more time, I can power through or be a little more leisurely with feature articles or longer magazine pieces. On a typical weekend, I might read anything from a new scientific discovery to a trend piece on work life to a profile of a newsmaker. As I read, I may circle a name that would make for a possible good guest, and then I bring that in for my producers to consider.

Reading is also a tool that can help deepen your relationships with friends or colleagues. I've found that when I show an interest in others' work, people tend to respond very well. You could offer to read over a draft presentation to make sure it is all set for a big meeting, and send a note of compliment afterward. Even better, say the praise in public in front of other colleagues. We all need a little boost once in a while, to feel like we are on the right track. Encouragement from colleagues is often returned. (I say "often" because sometimes it isn't and you just have to decide to choose to be kind for yourself—not for them—and let that be the reward.) If you show a habit of being kind, it will come back in positive ways to you. The opposite is also true—if you're sarcastic or mean, even just once, no one will forget it. And that can come back to hurt you. Think of it like this: Work karma. Karma works!

Another one of my favorite habits is to share articles with colleagues that I come across in my daily reading, which often have nothing to do with our work. You can do this with all sorts of people: Have colleagues that are interested in fly-fishing? Text that link. You remember that a boss's teen has a project on the Electoral College coming up? Send him an email. Know a friend struggling with childcare issues and see an article with helpful advice from another mom that's been there, too? Print it out and set it on their desk with a little note. This works with articles about a new Netflix series, feature pieces on a favorite band's upcoming new album release, a sports team's exciting new draft pick, or the dietary habits of the South American coatimundi. It's simple! And people appreciate it.

Don't forget, you can do this for yourself, too! I find note-to-self emails very helpful. But I know it's not for everyone. If emailing articles to yourself drives you crazy and overflows your inbox, you can also use apps like Pocket to help organize reads you want to save for later.

This reminds me of my friend's sons. They recently went on a vacation and were sitting in the airport lounge when their dad bought them a newspaper. After a bit, one of them looked up with a major discovery: "Look, Dad—it's like the whole Internet printed out for you to read!"

ACCURACY WINS THE RACE—NEVER FAKE IT

Part of all our work is being called on. This means being asked a series of questions and being expected to know or to be able to find an answer.

There's always a temptation to guess, estimate, or fake like you know the answer because you think it will make you look smarter or more prepared, or possibly help you avoid the boss's ire or impatience. But you must never ever do that.

Take, for example, being in a breaking news situation. The worst thing in the news business is passing on information to viewers that isn't correct. Something that is a maybe should never be said on air as a fact. If an anchor asks the producers, "Was it four or five people in the building?" and they don't know, they don't guess and say four. They say, "We are confirming right now." And then they double-check and confirm. I can't stress this strongly enough. This is good advice for every field, not just news.

Remember: your boss doesn't expect you to know all the answers. She expects you to know how to *find* the answers. So, get used to saying, "I'm not sure, but I will find out immediately." Or, "I believe I know, but let me double-check to make sure I'm getting you accurate information." They'll be so grateful that you aren't just running with something you're not sure of, possibly putting them in a bad spot. Don't be afraid to ask for direction if you don't know how to find out. (Of course, if you were supposed to have the answer a week ago, you better get your rear in gear.)

A friend of mine had a boss who was a sponge for information; any stray fact would stick in his mind. He picked up on anything that was said, even while he was reading through a speech or going through paperwork. This nearly got her in trouble one time.

Once, on their way to a speech, she told him a statistic that she'd read in the morning paper. She wasn't even sure he was listening. She was mainly trying to fill the silence.

Then, during the speech, her boss used that stat, and then in front of a crowd of hundreds of doctors, he pointed at my friend and said, "Isn't that right?"

She nodded but panicked. After the speech, she ran to the car to grab the paper to double-check. Fortunately, she was right. But she learned an important lesson that day.

That's why you should never tell your boss anything casually unless you *know* it to be true.

Along this line: start building your arsenal of fact-checking resources—whether it be online, through a reference library or book collection, or with a real live person (how novel!). You should also develop a system for storing information in an organized way, so that you can easily call things back up. If your boss is a heavy user of email, make electronic folders and be meticulous about keeping them updated.

One of the best feelings as a supervisor is when you start to ask for something and your employee says, "I have it right here," or, "I know where I can find that." Try not to have to ask your boss to resend something to you, but also don't be so afraid to ask that you waste hours looking for something that should be easy to find. Your goal should be to be considered a trusted source of information gathering. That makes you more reliable and valuable. (And you won't need dance lessons.)

DON'T BE A KNOWLEDGE HOARDER

And once you've gained a significant amount of knowledge, you have a leg up on the competition. What should you do with it?

Knowledge is power. But using that power against your peers or even junior staffers will not advance your station.

One of the best tips I know is to share what you know with others. That's a great way to build smart allies. Other people getting smarter does not make you dumber.

People in power tend to hoard their knowledge. And it's a universal issue. Once, when we visited Mercy Ships in Benin, the director of nursing told me about their education system for local health-care workers. She said the head doctor at the main hospital was quite a good physician, but he wouldn't teach anyone else what he knew because he thought it would diminish his power. The Mercy Ships nurse said that through experience, they'd seen that women are more willing to teach others what they learn because it will help the entire group if they can take better care of their patients.

Knowledge is power. Sharing it is empowering.

Section #4: Learn to love yourself (Justin Bieber taught us this)

Carry yourself with confidence

FIND YOUR STRONG VOICE—THEN USE IT

This brings me to something really important. Every single one of us needs to find our strong voice and use it.

What do I mean by that? Well, think about young people that use "up-talking" in their everyday speech.

It is so annoying—and to me it screams lack of credibility. Up-talking is where the last word of every sentence is in a higher octave, sometimes with a shakiness that's supposed to sound...cool? Ambivalent? Whatever it is meant to sound like, believe me that you will not get hired, promoted, or considered for big assignments if you talk like that. It sounds whiny, unsophisticated, and unsure. Like, it doesn't sound confident? Or strong? I feel like maybe it's a defense mechanism? (You get the idea.)

There's also the weird vocal fry, where someone sounds like they've been out all night and thinks it sounds cool to talk that way all the time. You are not Demi Moore or Jennifer Lawrence, and you can't pull this off. Tired, apathetic, dripping with weariness, vocalized from the back of the throat. Let me tell you, it doesn't inspire confidence.

Women also have to face the fact that their voices are usually in a higher register than male voices (unless you're channeling Elizabeth Holmes). And there's something about a lower register that commands more attention and respect. This is especially true in media. I have had to train myself to speak in a lower register, drawing more from my diaphragm than from up in my chest. Once I got the hang of it, I realized that it doesn't take much effort and that it does make a difference. I don't need to sound like Trace Adkins, but I don't want to sound like Adam Levine, either.

If you have a bad habit of up-talking, vocal fry, or being very... mousy...in your speech, there are ways to change it.

Try recording yourself during a meeting and listen to how it sounds. (Warning: everyone hates the sound of their own voice—unless you're Piers Morgan. I can barely stand to listen to or watch myself on television. I'd rather crawl under the table! But I know that I don't up-talk or use a vocal fry, that's for sure.)

You can also give yourself one week to try to break yourself of any bad habits. (This includes saying "like" over and over. It's, like... annoying, especially to older executives—and by older, I mean me or anyone over thirty.)

Also, choose a few women that you admire and listen to their voices. See if you can match their register while still being yourself. That can help trick your mind into getting you to improve your speaking voice. For me, I've always loved the sound of Diane Sawyer's voice—classy and gracious, while still being authoritative. She is someone I've enjoyed listening to and learning from over the years.

For those of you who are managers of young people and have noticed this problem, it is really important to gently and privately point it out. Most young people have no idea that they're doing something with their speech patterns that is holding them back—besides, all of their friends talk that way, too.

The good news is these habits can be broken—I've seen it happen—and it's incumbent upon women in the workplace to help each other. There are many obstacles to success and the competition for the best jobs is fierce—don't let your voice be a barrier to achievement.

LEADING BY EXAMPLE

Leadership is not necessarily a role that is assigned to you. You become a leader because you've taken action to lead something—such as a project, a decision-making exercise, or an event. People want leaders in their lives. The best way to become a leader is to jump in, take a chance, be a good listener, make decisions, and fill a void. If you can demonstrate the qualities of someone that should be listened to and followed, you'll *earn* the title of "leader."

Part of being a good leader is surrounding yourself with good people, especially when you're in a position to hire those people.

Find the most talented, most knowledgeable, and strongest people possible and add them to your team. Make sure to hire people who know more than you do. You don't want to always be the smartest woman in the room—you want to be the woman who gathers the smartest people together. And then listen to your team. Truly give them your undivided attention. Give them room to run. Show that you trust their judgment. Don't hog all the time with the top executives. Provide the opportunities to keep them interested and to assure them they are valued. Explain gently if you disagree with them, so that you don't chill a conversation or make someone feel they can't come to you with suggestions that you may not like but really need to hear. It's up to you to create that environment, and if you do all those things, you'll be a very good leader.

I recommend reading some books on leadership—there are so many. One of my favorites is *Decision Points*, by George W. Bush (naturally!). What I like most about the book is that the former president takes fourteen decisions he's made in his life and gives the reader a 360-degree view of all the inputs to the decision—the information he had at the time, the experts he listened to, and the citizens he heard from. He explains all of that so that you can understand how he came to the decision. You may read it and think that you'd decide differently. Fine. Good. That's all right. His point is not that you should agree with every decision he made, but that you should understand the decision-making process: what went into it and how he came to that conclusion.

Good leaders are calm when mistakes are made. Keep everything in perspective and don't lose your cool unnecessarily. And if it's you who made the mistake, own up to it, apologize quickly, and then take all the steps needed to fix it.

Remember, too, that great leaders don't always try to get the credit for something a team has done. Share the credit and you'll end up getting a lot more out of your team in the long run. I remember once when President Bush oversaw an operation to free some hostages—many of them American—in Colombia. I was there when he got the call from the CIA director that the mission was successful. I said that was great news and asked him what I could tell the press. We could always use a good-news story in the press office. But President Bush insisted that all due credit go to the Colombian president for the cooperation and courage to accomplish the mission. Plus, the president was trying to get the House Democrats to pass a free trade agreement with Colombia—to deepen our ties with a great ally in the region. The Democrats were holding it up, using the fight against narco-terrorists as the reason. Eventually, that agreement got signed. And I always remember that moment of a leader deflecting praise for a pretty awesome rescue effort to advance the process of achieving a goal. Keep that in mind—what really matters? The accomplishment or the credit?

Leadership is both something you already have inside of you and something that can be learned. Make an investment in learning about great leaders and their characteristics, so that you can keep adding to your capabilities.

Small tip: pick one of the innumerable aphorisms on leadership and memorize it. When in doubt, default to it. I say this because there is so much advice out there on how to lead, and it all overlaps. It's hard to retain it all under pressure.

A good friend has a go-to leadership mantra from General George S. Patton: Don't tell people what to do. Tell them where you want to get, and let them surprise you with their ingenuity.

One of my favorites is from President Bush after the 9/11 attacks. I printed this and had it tacked to the wall in my office for years: We will not tire. We will not fail. Peace and freedom will prevail.

That became a mantra for me. In times of hope or worry, I'd

repeat it. To me, I was reminded to be focused on the goal, and to trust in liberty.

Find your quote—you'll be amazed what's out there. You'll find something that speaks directly to you and it will stay with you forever.

INVITED FOR A REASON

Once you move past your starting position at a company and receive more responsibility, you'll find yourself invited to more meetings. And perhaps, if it's allowed, your boss will send you in her place since she can't be in two places at once. If you're going to get a seat at the table, you have to use it wisely.

First, make sure you do the reading ahead of time, and find out where your boss stands on the issue at hand and whether she needs you to take notes or to make a point. Bring pen and paper to take a lot of notes, then type them up into a smart summary for her to review (do this without being asked).

If she wants you to speak up, you have to do it with a clear voice and direct eye contact. I remember once being asked to go to a meeting for someone, and before I left her office, my boss said, "And I don't expect you to be quiet as a mouse in there. I'm sending you to the meeting for a reason."

Now, that might not seem like that big a deal, getting to go to a meeting. But it is showing trust in you. And if you handle that well, more responsibility will come your way. Have your point, say it clearly, and stay focused.

You also may be asked to attend a more public event, outside of the office. A dinner, perhaps, where you need to know which fork to use and that the bread plate is always on your left. This is a good time to decline any alcoholic beverages or to accept just one glass of wine and sip it slowly. Don't let an opportunity like this be ruined by drinking too much and getting sloppy (especially if you've not eaten all day!).

You'll likely not know anyone else at the table, so have a few go-to introductory phrases, which can be anything from small talk about the weather or a question about the honoree or keynote speaker. If you're really stuck and the silence feels a little awkward, a good icebreaker is to ask your dining partners about their lives and careers. "Where did you grow up?" is a great question—maybe you have been to their hometown or have always wanted to visit. Another is "How long have you been with your company?" If the conversation is going well, you could also ask them for advice—people love to give it (your author included)—on topics from your career to suggestions for a good book. And if you've been doing your reading and listening to podcasts, you'll always have something interesting to point out or add to the conversation.

Before leaving for the evening, make sure to shake everyone's hands and thank them for the pleasure of spending the dinner in their company. Exchange contact information if appropriate, and then the next morning send a note saying how it was great to meet them and you hope your paths cross again. Because they just might! It's a small world.

TALK LESS; LISTEN MORE

Listeners are the ones that really solve conflicts and problems. They're often the most respected people within a company and among their friends.

It is easier said than done. I'm a talker, and a fast one. When Peter and I first met and were married not long afterward, he would sometimes ask me to slow down and repeat what I'd said. I'd get a little irritated: "I have a lot to say. Keep up!" (As you may have guessed, he's a patient man.)

While I've learned to slow down a bit, it's really in the last several years that I've discovered the true value of listening more than I talk. (Outside of the shows, of course. Dead air on your television is a ratings killer. But there's not much chance of that on *The Five*...)

One of the main reasons to keep quiet is because you not only learn more, but you'll also gain more respect. People very much appreciate when they are heard. If you're in a meeting and want to get your point of view in, write down a quick note with your question or thought, and that way you won't forget what you were going to say but you also won't interrupt someone while they're making their points. You'll also find that, very often, they get to your question anyway. Then you get to be the mysterious nontalking person in the room who everyone is intrigued by (no need to tell them later you were mulling where to get lunch).

Here's a tip to prevent yourself from interrupting others: literally put your hand over your mouth (subtly—don't clamp it over like you have a big secret you're dying to spill). This cuts your tendency to weigh in while someone else is talking. It's worth a try.

Being an active listener means giving feedback to whoever is speaking—by making eye contact, nodding along, sitting still, and asking questions. People know if you're not paying attention—it's distracting and rude.

Listening also gives you an edge over others—if you're quiet and observing the entire scene rather than itching to make a point or sighing while someone else finishes an argument you disagree with, you'll be turned to as the one people want to hear from.

As the old saying goes, you have two ears and one mouth—use them in the proper proportions.

WRITE IT DOWN . . . WITH A PEN . . . ON AN ACTUAL PIECE OF PAPER

Back in the old days of journalism, a press secretary used to invite a few reporters to the office for a "pen and pad." This is where journalists could come and get some information and background, maybe an on-the-record quote or two, that would help them with news that was going to break soon (like the introduction of new health-care legislation, or a look ahead to a foreign trip).

Most journalists can write very quickly with a pen—deciphering their penmanship can be another story. Tape recorders are often used to ensure that nothing is missed and to provide backup in case someone challenges the accuracy of a quote.

In come the laptop and the phone. Now the pen and pad has become a place where people are typing wildly on their computers or onto their screens.

On occasion when I'm in meetings or doing interviews, I get so distracted by the noise or by someone typing on their phone that I start to wonder, Are they paying attention to what's being said? Or are they mindlessly scrolling through Instagram, shopping online, or playing Scrabble with friends? Then I lose my train of thought. Why do I think it seems rude for me to ask, "Are you paying attention to this?" Being on your phone during a meeting or presentation—now *that's* rude!

And yet regularly you see people miss things in meetings because they're busy on their phones. (A friend that read an early draft of this book wrote in the margins, "This is so true—I [expletive] hate it when I'm trying to get to a point and one of my people starts futzing with their phone.") So, you see, I'm not the only one. This really is a problem.

When you glance at your phone, your attention is pulled away. And whoever is speaking notices. Maybe it's your boss. Or your boss's boss. Or a colleague that's doing a presentation. This is irritating and unfocused.

I recommend getting in the habit of taking a notebook and pen to every meeting you go to. That way you're sure not to miss something, and the principal or supervisor doesn't have to wonder if you're paying attention. And if you don't have a piece of paper, ask if it is okay for you to take notes on your phone. You'll get a yes and a nod of gratitude for asking. Think of how mad your mom would be if you came home for a family dinner and were on your phone the entire time. That's how your boss feels, too.

Plus, carrying a notebook into your boss's office can help prevent mistakes. Imagine you're at a restaurant with a large group, and the waitress comes over and doesn't write down anyone's order. Immediately you get a sinking feeling that she's going to forget that John doesn't want mayonnaise on his sandwich and the dinner salad was with blue cheese, not ranch.

Well, that happens at work, too. Let's say you are called into your boss's office and she gives you a list of five things to do. You nod, thinking you have it all. But you miss something that your boss just rattled off, and two days later she asks, "Did you forget to cancel that appointment? Why are they calling me now?" or, "The client says the package didn't arrive—please tell me you remembered to mail it yesterday."

Your sinking feeling will be because you didn't write it all down. Dropping the ball results in a loss of confidence in you.

There's an easy fix—get a new notebook and start using a pen again. It makes you more reliable and look more professional. People giving instructions feel better if they see you writing something down—it gives them confidence that you're getting the message. Then make sure to refer back to the notes, cross off the to-do items as you get them done, and then check back in to confirm everything was taken care of. Don't be a note taker that doesn't follow through.

If you absolutely must take your phone to a meeting, make sure that it is on silent mode—completely silent. That means for notifications of any sort. But if you can, leave your phone at your desk.

If you do this, you'll stand out from everyone else because very few people do this anymore. Trust me and give it a try.

THANK YOU VERY MUCH, MA'AM

I'm a proponent of handwritten thank-you notes, written on decent stationery and sent in the actual mail ... with a stamp and everything.

I remember seeing a young woman who'd had an interview earlier in the day and asking her if she'd written a thank-you note yet. She said, "Don't you think that would make it look like I was trying too hard for the job?" I said, "No, it will not look like that. Besides, do you want the job?" Yes. There's your answer.

So, if you ever find yourself asking, "Should I send a thank-you note to ... ?" the answer is always yes. Always.

Section #5: Be proud of your cyber self

Sent from my iPhone—quick tips for email etiquette and clear communication online

TAKE CONTROL OF TEXTS AND EMAILS

Communication is the most important thing at any office and in any relationship. All problems can usually be boiled down to a lack of communication or a miscommunication.

That's increasingly true with how much we are communicating now. When we used to have to send a letter by mail or a press release by fax, there were fewer chances for mistakes. But now our fingers fly across keyboards so fast that we're apt to make some errors.

A few suggestions:

- Find out how your boss likes to communicate. Is it email or text? A mix of both? When does she prefer a text over an email? Or do you need to send a text to make sure she looks at her email? Ask her how she wants to share information to ensure a smoother experience and prevent frustration.
- Always use a clear subject line for each email. Do not add a new topic in an email chain that is under a completely different subject head. For example, if you have an email chain going about some travel plans to a conference in two weeks, and then you ask, "By the way, do you want me to cancel this afternoon's interview since you are now wanted in the boardroom at 3:00 p.m.?" your boss would have a right to be irritated...plus, chances are she may miss that email altogether. And saying, "But I emailed you earlier," is not going to cut it when she realizes she's double booked. Don't let things get lost in the shuffle.
- Never reply in anger or sarcasm (no matter how good the zinger might be). If you are hot under the collar, draft the note, then take a few breaths or go for a coffee. Come back and delete the message and start over. Don't let your temper cause you unnecessary problems. Besides, when you think about it for a while, you'll come up with a better response than if you punch back before you've thought it through.
- Only reply to all when it's necessary to have clear communication. Avoid the frivolous thread-adding to a large group.

- Never reply to an email and add someone with a note that says "looping in James" without first finding out whether the original sender is okay with that. There may be a good reason that that person was left off the email in the first place. No need to cause a problem by rushing to loop someone in.

   Let me give you an example that will ensure you do not do this: A friend of mine was once on a group email that was long and included a lot of tasks for others. Along the way, one of the recipients added another co-worker because that person was responsible for one of the assignments.

   The problem was the person who looped the other co-worker in didn't bother reading the entire email, and the person who was added was punched in the gut when he read that the last line of the email was a recommendation to "fire him." What a terrible way to learn that you're losing your job—imagine how bad he felt, and how much unnecessary anger and confusion was caused just by adding someone without asking permission first. (Also, it's probably better to never write that someone should be fired in an email in the first place!)

- Be sparing in your emails and texts to your boss. If you feel overwhelmed by email, I've found that the fewer you send, the fewer you get. Unsubscribe to emails you don't need anymore. And put personal email on another device.

   Being known as an efficient emailer rather than a prolific one is a good thing. You don't want to undercommunicate, but overcommunicating can get annoying, and important messages can get lost in the mix.

   As a manager, think about how your staff deals with your email habits. When I started *The Daily Briefing* show, I realized that on evenings and weekends, I was emailing my staff

way too often. I am constantly reading news and checking tweets so that I don't miss anything, and I'd forward
way too many ideas for them to keep up with. So, I started
something new—on Saturdays, I open a new email and put
anything in there I find worth considering for the week's
shows. Then on Sunday in the late afternoon, I review that
draft email and usually delete at least half of the suggestions.
Then I send the team just one email with all my thoughts in
one place. It's working for me, and I think my staff appreci-
ates it. (I can't imagine how annoying my previous habit was
for them—I apologize!)

- Tidy up the inbox, too. Take ten minutes to keep your inbox
  clean—delete all those emails you don't need (like the ones
  trying to get you to buy another pair of black yoga pants;
  trust me—you don't need any more). Ideally, I like to have
  under twenty emails in my inbox. That makes me feel like I
  have a handle on things.

  When I get over a hundred emails in there, I feel uncomfortable, like I'm being chased by a monster in a nightmare.
  I feel like I'll never outrun it if I don't constantly delete,
  respond, and file emails.

  A friend of mine has a unique system of handling the
  flood of emails that come in.

  He has two folders at the top of his inbox—"To Do
  Today" and "Don't Panic." The "To Do Today" folder
  helps him make sure that he doesn't forget something that's
  important or that has a deadline—he clears out that folder
  before wrapping up his day.

  The Don't Panic folder is for those emails that require
  a longer, more complex response. It's especially for emails
  that go on and on and are complicated in their direction

and requests—the ones that make you wish you'd never opened them. I liked this idea because I often leave emails like that marked "Unread" and that means I have a harder time clearing my inbox. Though I might name mine "Punish the Sender."

Going back a few decades, there was a time-management suggestion that a piece of paper should touch your desk only once—and that was a good way to keep your desk clear of clutter. Plus, it forced you to be more efficient. See if you can do that with emails, too. And when you get to "No Mail" one day, you will feel so good. Take a screenshot and aim to get there once a month. For those of you comfortable with 25,000 emails in your inbox, the only thing I can suggest is to declare email bankruptcy and delete all of them and start over. Short of that, I'm of no help to you! (But archive them. You never know…)

- How you compose an email is very important. If an email is too long and not formatted well, no one is going to read it. If the email is incomplete and leaves the recipients with more questions than answers, you failed. A friend of mine recently started a new job. Her new boss asked what time they should schedule calls. She surprised him by saying, "You shouldn't need to call me. If you're calling me, that means that I've not given you something you need." She didn't want to take up his time with a call, and she set an expectation that she would make sure he had what he needed without worry. I'm absolutely in favor of actual conversations, but for a busy boss, this kind of support is invaluable. Saving your supervisor time is much appreciated. Fifteen minutes saved is like finding a twenty-dollar bill in your pocket!
- Take some time and care to write a good message.

I used to write a "night note" for the senior staff of the White House that would give them a recap of the press office's day and whatever they needed to be prepared for when they saw the newspapers in the morning. I took pride in writing notes that were short enough to be read by a busy person and clear enough to not make anyone confused. I found that if I took the time to draft a good email, I saved everyone some time and I was a more effective communicator. I called it my nightly ounce of panic prevention. (Others call it "insomnia.")

This is similar advice to what I wrote in *And the Good News Is....* One of my current producers knows that I put a premium on good email communication and sent me a TikTok of a young millennial woman struggling over how to end an email she'd just written. In the background you hear the song "Human" by The Human League. Finally, after a lot of agonizing decision making, the young woman changes "Thanks." to "Thanks!" and presses Send as relief washes over her. I laughed. Of course, I don't want email composition to become so all consuming as to be paralyzing. Just do your thing well—and use an exclamation point if you really want to.

- If you use voice to text, be sure to check your messages carefully before you hit Send. I can't even write in this book how many times I've seen mistakes in emails and texts as a result of this feature—and some of them can be quite...unfortunate. Even profane!

  Peter has had more mistakes than we can count. His English accent is picked up differently on his iPhone. The results are quite hilarious. Here's one: After a hurricane wrecked coastal parts of South Carolina, where we used to have a home, our friends went by to check on our property.

"All clear! But there's a little black cat that's hiding under your motorcycle," they texted. Peter knew our neighbor had a cat fitting that description, so he voice texted asking if she had her little black cat with her. Except the voice text didn't write "cat"...It wrote...(pardon me) "cock" (red-faced embarrassed emoji).

Thankfully, our neighbor realized what happened and assured Peter that yes, she had everything...um...under control. We had a good laugh about it, but Peter has never lived that one down. (We settled that one out of court.)

While these can make for great stories later, they're not so funny when they happen. Protect yourself and give each voice text, especially work-related ones, a once-over before you hit Send.

- Set some time limits on when you'll respond to emails. Many businesses are international, so if you don't put boundaries on your day, you could answer emails around the clock. A young friend of mine who lives on the East Coast mentioned how tired she was because she was up at 4:00 a.m. responding to emails that had come in from Europe. I asked, "Why are you doing that? Was it anything urgent?" Not really, no, she said. I told her that she must stop checking her phone before 6:00 a.m. and to put it in a drawer across the room if she needed to avoid the temptation. I told her, "Do you think you look strong and in control when you're responding to emails before dawn? Do you think anyone in Europe would respond to your messages in the middle of the night? No! So, promise me right now that you'll stop." She promised. Though I doubt she put her phone in a drawer!

- Finally, reintroduce yourself to the actual telephone. Often a message can be more clearly and quickly delivered by just picking up the phone and calling someone. It's so efficient. Thank you, Alexander Graham Bell! (Just google him.)

EXCLAMATION POINTS!!!

Take this to heart: exclamation points should be used sparingly. If they're overused, especially in professional writing and emails, they lose their effect. Specifically, I really don't like exclamation points in subject lines of emails—unless it's an emergency, don't do that. If you're a boss, think about what signals you're sending—do you need an exclamation point that will cause your team to have unnecessary anxiety? And if you're trying to convey urgency or emphasize something, try using stronger language.

An observation: an overreliance on exclamation points can be a sign of insecurity. It often reads as frivolous. To me, it is the grammatical equivalent of up-speak—and in my experience, it is almost exclusively women who do it. I get it—an exclamation point can signal that you're not mad that someone hasn't yet responded to a question with a deadline. It says, "I'm nice! Truly! Like me, please!" Pay attention to emails you get from people you admire, your managers, and your role models. Do they use a lot of exclamation points? I doubt it. This is a habit you can easily break. Here's a tip: when closing out an email, instead of writing "Thanks! Dana" try saying, "Thanks—Dana." It is a subtle signal but one that shows that you're calm and in control.

And this leads to another thing. Emojis. To use or not to use in emails. I've come around a bit on them. I think they can work well—especially if you're trying to lighten a mood. Look, humans have been using symbols and pictures to communicate with each other forever. I wouldn't send a formal email with an emoji to a supervisor, but among your team and with younger staffers, if it makes sense to send a thumbs-up or a smiley face, why not? Just make sure the emoji won't be taken the wrong way—stick with the basic, safe emojis and stay away from, um...the weird ones (I know you know what I mean).

RECONSIDER YOUR OUT-OF-OFFICE REPLY

I am not a fan of the out-of-office reply setting. I realize it's useful if you'll be gone a week or more, and if you'll truly be unreachable and not checking your emails (which these days only happens if you're climbing Everest or on a nuclear submarine...and probably not even there). If that's the case, by all means use it to let people know you won't be getting back to them right away and who they should contact in the meantime.

However, we live in a time when people are working evenings and weekends (more on that and the elusive "work-life balance" in a later chapter), so it isn't unusual to respond to an email that comes in during "off" hours. There are very few off hours in this competitive world, and if you want to set yourself apart, that means working smartly, efficiently, even when you're not in the office.

If you're going to be checking your email regularly anyway, why put an out-of-office reply notification on? And if you do plan on taking a break from email, make sure to let your boss know.

I especially don't like the messages that explain that you're away for two weeks because you've worked so hard and deserve it. That might be true, but we don't need to know that. We're all working hard—we all deserve time off. And please don't tell us where you went. I'm in my cubicle, fending off clients and answering *your* emails. I don't need to be reminded that you're sipping something out of a coconut in Fiji. Part of being considered as the go-to, reliable, must-have employee means being available, even reasonably so when you're not in the office. Unless it is necessary, don't use the out-of-office reply option.

SOCIAL MEDIA DILEMMA

Young professionals have had to deal with social media their entire careers, whereas it was new to me as I was departing the White House. On my last day as press secretary in January 2009, I didn't even have a Twitter account or a Facebook page. All of that has changed, of course (especially when I was shown how to post pictures of my dog, which remains the highest and best use of all social media).

There's no shortage of advice about social media use and how it can affect your career.

You are completely in charge of your social media—you decide what to post and how to interact. You can't blame mistakes on anyone else. You have to utilize these tools wisely.

A few good rules of thumb:

- Don't post something that might make your boss or future employer cringe. Ask yourself, "Does this post of my excessive night out with the girls convey a message that says, 'This person should be in charge of our main client, public interfacing, or crisis management' or does it convey, 'This girl has major issues and probably needs to dial back on #RoséAllDay'?" If you ever question *whether* to post something, *don't*. It is impossible to unsee something that makes you wonder what in the world that person was thinking when she posted that picture.
- Use privacy settings and consider having a public page and a private one. That way you can protect yourself a little if you're more of a prolific poster. Only a valid search warrant can penetrate this. If that happens, you likely have bigger problems.
- Consider what you like, retweet, or comment on. There are times when I read a tweet that is super funny to me, but I realize that if I like it, that could come back to haunt me. I've

learned to play it safe on social media by witnessing others pay a price.

I did have one viral tweet that wasn't embarrassing for me work-wise, but funny-embarrassing overall. It was Super Bowl 2019 and we were invited to a neighbor's for the game. I decided I'd make queso in my Crock-Pot, and I tried a recipe I found online for queso made like at Chili's, the restaurant. It burbled for hours before we left for the party. Once there, I put it on the table with the other snacks, set out some tortilla chips, and snapped a picture for Twitter. I wrote, "I made queso." That was it.

Or so I thought. About two hours later, I checked my phone. I had multiple texts from friends asking me if I'd seen Twitter. My stomach dropped. My blood ran cold for a moment. Had I done something wrong? Bad? Was I being attacked?

Nope! I was being ridiculed. Apparently my queso looked a little...gross...and this tweet was now flying around the world with celebrities and chefs weighing in. I started trending on Twitter (a first for me!).

The queso tweet kept us going at Fox News for a few days. Chili's even sent me a queso bomber jacket and defended me—they said I followed the recipe perfectly (which I doubt; mine ended up looking like industrial runoff, but it tasted good).

That was my one and only brush with Internet fame. So I'm packing up my Velveeta and staying home now.

I could have been even more famous on Instagram, however. But by the grace of God—and because he knew I'd kill him—Peter wasn't recording at the time. Here's what happened. One summer evening, we lugged paddleboards down to a lake and brought Jasper along with us. I thought it would be fun to put him on a board and get some pictures. Jasper prefers just to wade along the shoreline hunting for fish.

But with enough treats, Peter got him on his board and away we went. Jasper looked like a captain of a boat—not having to lift a paw to paddle. Peter did all the work.

I hustled to return to the beach before they did so that I could take a picture. Then I wanted one with Jasper. Well, let me tell you—getting Jasper back on the board was tough. He wanted to fish instead. We finally got him on but then had a hard time getting him to look at the camera. He was dying to get back into the water. To make matters worse, Peter's phone was set to a timer so every picture took three seconds longer than usual to save. The whole time I just stood there trying to look natural, like I was out in the middle of the lake with my dog on a beautiful summer evening and didn't my life look great.

Finally, Peter got enough photo options and said, "Okay."

Well, *Okay* is Jasper's word for "You are free to go now."

And boy did he. Jasper lunged into the water, shoving the paddleboard way back. Splash! I lost my balance and did a face plant into the water. My pride was hurt, my wrist was sore, and I was soaking wet. I looked up and could see Peter was trying so hard not to laugh. Why had he said Okay?! (Now that I think about it, I wonder . . .)

I saw the humor in it. Here I am, giving advice to young women about not trying to be a hero on social media, and I got caught posing for a photo that went all wrong.

The only saving grace was that Peter didn't get it on video!

- Ask yourself if the social media you're using is serving you well. Is it sucking up all your time? Is it keeping you from having better friendships? Is it hurting your chances of a promotion or keeping you from getting the new job you want? What would happen if you deleted an app from your phone? Do you really need multiple exercise apps that count you down from a three-minute plank? (One will do.)

What I've heard from young people that have pulled the plug on multiple social media platforms and instead just use one, usually Instagram, is that they feel less stressed. So, if it would benefit your well-being and your professional life, maybe streamline your online time as a good way to declutter your day. (It may also keep you from walking into traffic.)

I remember being impressed with someone I recently interviewed who didn't have any social media. That made me wonder—was he trying to hide something? Or was that just good judgment? During our discussion, I could tell that he didn't believe it was useful to him. This showed me that he could withstand peer pressure, manage his time well, and that I wouldn't have to worry that something he posted would reflect negatively on him, me, or the company. It was a net positive.

Now, I like social media for a lot of reasons (aside from pet pics). Over the years, I've tried to strike a balance on informing myself and promoting my appearances and commentary. But if it all went away overnight, my life would be exactly the same (except I'd have a lot more time to focus on Peter or read a book instead of scrolling through Twitter and Instagram).

Think about that. Are you using social media in a way that enhances your life? Or has it taken over your life? When it starts to be overwhelming, stressful, and all consuming, keeps you from face-to-face interactions with real people, or when it is holding you back professionally, then you should consider cutting back...possibly altogether.

HELP OLDER (THAT MEANS ME!) EMPLOYEES WITH TECHNOLOGY

You may not feel like it right now, but young people have several advantages over the "elders" at the office. With youth comes boundless energy and enthusiasm, fewer responsibilities, and an ability to go out all night and not suffer the next day from a raging hangover. (However, I don't recommend this on the weeknights!)

One of your greatest strengths is your adaptability to using new technology. With the rate of innovation today, it's hard for companies big and small to keep up. Your talents in this area are your advantage, so be willing to help other employees, including your bosses, to learn how to pick up new tools without grudge or frustration. As soon as you lose patience with someone and tell them to move away from the keyboard or device, you lose some of your tech magic.

Instead of throwing up your hands, take a deep breath and try again. Eventually, the office dinosaur will get it. You'll be rewarded as a problem solver, and you might even help make the company more efficient. Saving time is saving money, and when a company has more money, they can afford to pay workers (yeah, you) more or increase benefits.

And this goes for helping others do things that have nothing to do with work. Let's say someone's grandson lives across the country and they want to be able to connect on social media or via a new communications app. Set it up for them and they'll never forget it.

Bottom line: you have power over your office mates from the twentieth century with your technical capabilities. Don't lord this over anyone—just use it wisely. (Also, how do I make those fancy graphics on my Insta story? Tell me later...)

Section #6: Friendship is a two-way street

What goes around comes around

MAKE FRIENDS; DON'T GOSSIP

I have a friend who mentors young people in Florida—kids who have been in trouble with the law but are trying to put themselves on a steadier path. The first thing he says to them is, "If you introduce me to your five best friends, I'll tell you where you'll be in five years."

At first they'll balk, thinking this is ridiculous. How can this older guy know anything about their future based on a few guys they hang out with? But he told me he's never been wrong. And within a couple of mentoring sessions, he said they absolutely understand what he means about the importance of who you surround yourself with. He believes they know it in their gut anyway, or maybe they've heard it from their moms and just didn't want to listen. He said it's gratifying to see the young men he's mentored turn into leaders who make better choices for themselves.

The lesson he's teaching these guys is that you should surround yourself with good people who add meaning, joy, laughter, and support to your life. You should extricate yourself from folks who only take energy from you, drag down your moods, or put you in risky situations. That doesn't mean you only hang out with people you agree with: not at all. It does mean establishing strong relationships with people who have good judgment, positive outlooks, and strong character.

Think about that right now. Who is in your group of friends? Do you have a good social circle? Are you supported in your goals? Are you free to be yourself and do you enjoy some good laughs when you're together? Do you need to add someone to your group, or even slowly back away from someone who may be a drain on your energy?

This is a good way to approach your work friends as well. All of us have varying degrees of friendships at work—some people you just wave to in the hallways, others you have to partner with on specific projects, and still others you might go out for coffee or even dinner with on occasion.

I advocate being friends with as many people as possible in your life. At least be friendly to everyone. What you give is what you get—you want people to be nice to you, too. That doesn't mean everyone is going to be your best friend—but a little bit of effort to be kind to people at the office will help you gain a reputation as a good person to work with.

One complication to this is if you're hanging around with someone who is very negative at work or the purveyor of office gossip. That's not good for *your* daily work life, and it could hurt you when it comes to promotions. The bosses notice everything, or, if they don't see it, they hear about everything. Believe me. I laugh when I see young staffers who think their supervisors are clueless. They're not. Bosses are like parents—they have eyes in the back of their heads. If they see you causing problems, riling people up, or spreading rumors, they will cross you off their mental list for promotions, travel opportunities, or new challenges. And even if your work product is perfect, this can hurt you when it comes to your review.

If you think that you have made a bad choice in befriending someone who you didn't realize is a problem around the office, find a way to remove yourself gently from the situation. Come up with reasons to sidestep going to coffee and avoid hanging out at the cafeteria at the same time. Maybe you'll have to start eating lunch at your desk for a while. Pretend you're on the phone when they stop by to gossip or take on extra work until you can get out of that negative loop. Sometimes you make a bad call when it comes to judging someone's character. It happens. There are ways to get that behind you, and every experience like this helps you make better decisions in the future.

Let's take another possible scenario. Say you deal with a colleague who is a bully, aggressive, or mean-spirited to you or about others. You put up with it, or even try to be nice and placate them, because you're concerned that if you complain, you'll lose your job. First of all, realize that you don't have to be their friend. Being nice to them may encourage them to keep talking to you. You can be professional and get your work done without indulging them. And document instances of toxic behavior so that you have the evidence you need if it escalates to needing to go to management.

Another possible bad co-worker is someone on your team that tries to go behind your back or get an advantage over you. These people are the worst. And you have to get in front of them. Address it head-on with your manager. Chances are they know what's going on and don't like it any more than you do. And if you manage someone who tries to play politics, show them the door. Make an example out of them.

All of us have made a bad judgment call along the way when it comes to friends and people we hang out with at the office. This is especially true of that toxic asset in the pod—the one who complains about work, disrespects supervisors, and tries to get you to agree. And they're always a little too loud. This would be a good time to say less and to use your headphones more. Make yourself busier—take on an additional assignment, offer to run an errand or visit the client everyone is afraid of. Extricate yourself from the situation. Once you've gone through it, you'll be able to spot problem people and avoid making that mistake again.

MAKE FRIENDS, NOT JUST CO-WORKERS

The advice I give to every new staff member is to make friends with everyone they possibly can. That means broadly across the building and the organization—from the security guards to the mail room guys and gals to the executive assistants in the C-suite. Get to know people, not just your immediate co-workers in your cube pen.

And don't forget the IT department—that's a must! Learn their names, get to know them, say hello in the hallway, and recognize them during special occasions like birthdays and holidays. This will ensure that whenever you melt down your hard drive and accidentally click on malware (not that this has happened to me), your call will be returned first.

I also suggest that young staffers help new employees find their way around the office. I understand this is called "onboarding" now. I'm not much for HR jargon, but I get the concept. I have watched too many people show up to a new place of work and have no idea how to make a phone call, where to get more supplies, or even where the bathroom is. Always stop to help the new person, because you'll be the new person again one day, too. And because you took the time to learn their name and care for them, you'll have a fan for life.

And even a five-dollar Starbucks gift card at Christmas for a cleaner or mail room staff you see every day can cement your reputation as a thoughtful person (and will likely mean you never have to wonder where that package went).

SURPRISE SOMEONE; HELP YOURSELF

Try to find a way at least once a week to go over and beyond with an assignment.

Can you make your boss's life easier by getting in front of a problem so that she doesn't have to worry about it when she gets to the office? Can you take on extra work for a colleague who had a family emergency? And can you do all of this without asking for credit?

To me, if you can do this, it'll become a habit that over time is noticed as one of your qualities. You'll be referred to as the reliable one, the one to turn to when there's a problem, when something really needs to get done. You'll increase your job satisfaction and climb that ladder faster than your competition (and graciously, of course!).

Most people do the minimum at work. Even a little extra will make you stand out. (Just make sure it's appropriate. Showing up unannounced with homemade cupcakes at your boss's home may not be the best idea.)

MAKING THE BEST OF AN OPEN OFFICE PLAN

I'm not a fan of the open office plan (and I felt this way before the COVID-19 pandemic). I realize it makes sense for some teams working together to not have walls as barriers to brainstorming. And in the news business, it can help to have bureaus clustered together so they are able to see and hear one another clearly when a story is breaking.

But overall, I don't like them. I think people do better work when they have a little privacy. And who wants to be observed all the time anyway? No one wants to work in a zoo. Or watch an office mate paint their nails. That said, the rows of cubicles are here to stay for a while. So how can you best survive if this is the case where you work?

- Tidy up. You must try to keep your space as neat as possible. That means not having papers untidily stacked everywhere, four coffee cups scattered on your desk, and clutter that makes it look like it would be hard to find anything, let alone be productive. I suggest doing what my mom called a "five-minute pickup." This is where she would deploy my dad, sister, and me to pick up for five minutes—putting shoes and toys (in my case, books) away, placing our dog's toys back in his basket, gathering dishes from rooms and putting them in the dishwasher, hanging coats back in the closet, etc.

It's pretty impressive what you can get done in five minutes. If you make a commitment to doing this every day before you leave the office, you'll be able to hit the ground running the next morning. But if you leave a mess that builds up, you will not impress your boss the next time she walks by and your desk looks like a tornado hit a Staples. Five minutes a day is a worthy investment.

Some companies have a "clean-desk policy" whereby desks must be cleared at the end of the working day (this is very common in government—especially if you work with classified materials). Even if your company doesn't, it's a good idea for you to do this. Stand out by making it your own policy!

Let me add that being smart and tidy and responsible includes whatever you hang on your cubicle walls. Keep it classy and fun! You don't want people to wander by your desk and then whisper to each other, "Did you see what she had on her wall? What *was* that? Should we call the vice squad?"

This happened to one of my younger staffers at the White House. The West Wing had just been remodeled, with freshly painted walls and new carpet. Everything looked great. It had that new West Wing smell! (Don't ask.)

The decorator was giving a senior member of the White House a final tour after we'd all moved back in. My assistant press secretary had a tiny space, but hey hey hey—it was in the West Wing! She had a sliding pocket door for privacy but left it open most of the time. On her wall, she had a fancy bulletin board with pushpins holding up pictures with friends, programs from White House events (including one with the queen of England!), and the menu for the Navy Mess where we could order takeout for lunches at our desks.

When the tour came by, she was away from her office. The other press office staffers sitting nearby heard them remark on her bulletin board, saying, "What does she think this is, her *dorm room*?"

Well, my staffer never heard the end of it. We decided she needed a shag carpet and a mini beanbag to complete the look.

We laugh about it now—we've teased her for years. Now she just posts her pictures on everyone's dorm room—Instagram.

- Noises in the office are a big issue for me (but I'm a little weird that way). I'm overly sensitive to noise, so it affects me more than most people. But when you're in an open office plan, everyone can hear everything. How anyone can think straight is beyond me.

  Set your phone ringer to its lowest setting, eliminating the dings and bings, tweeting bird noises, and other such annoying sounds that come from electronic devices that alert you to yet another text or email that has been received. We don't need to hear a swoosh when you send a tweet or post a photo. Besides, if you're glued to your phones and computers all day—and you are—you're not going to miss anything, so you don't need these notifications. Save yourself and your neighbors from the relentless electronic noises that are assaulting us all day long. It has the added benefit of calming your nerves as well. (Okay, I'm making that up, but still give it a try!)

  In addition, moderate the volume at which you speak to colleagues and on the phone. If you need to have a rip-roarin' phone call because a vendor didn't deliver what you needed to a conference, find a private room where you can let loose. You don't want to subject other people to that.

And while it can be hard not to overhear conversations, try not to repeat something you've heard or to violate someone's confidentiality. Hopefully, they'll do the same for you.

And by the way: you can't sing. No, really. I know it sounds great in your head, but your unique rendering of "I Will Always Love You" is best left for the shower.

Also, use your earphones at your desk when you're on a call or listening to music while you work. This is not only courteous, but it's also a way to avoid accidentally playing unintentional or explicit music over your speakers. If your boss walks by and wants to talk, be sure to take out the Air-Pods before she starts talking—you don't want to miss anything. Plus, taking them out gives her the confidence that you're paying full attention to her.

- Respect others' privacy—and protect your own. The hardest part of an open floor plan is the lack of privacy for both you and your colleagues. Do what you need to do to keep your computer screen private, and don't forget to lock your computer screen before you walk away (this is a good habit to get into). Privacy is important for the company's security and yours as well. And it could avoid having the office "comedian" asking the boss for a 200 percent raise from your email.

CALL WITH SUPPORT

Another tip is that you should always call your friends on days when things aren't going their way. Let's say the boss yelled at them for something that wasn't their fault. Or they said something on air that was taken the wrong way or that if they had the chance to take it back, they would.

When things are tough for someone else, the tendency for most people is to back away. Perhaps it's too awkward to address it or you think it would be better not to mention it. I learned from President Bush the exact opposite. He said you always should call your friends on the days when no one else will. In fact, he told the AP and Reuters reporters that during his last week in office. They were surprised how often he and Bill Clinton had been in touch over his two terms— having lunch on occasion when the former president was in town to see Senator Clinton, or catching up by phone. He said, "I called him when there was a rough patch. Like when an Obama supporter suggested that Clinton was a racist during the hard-fought primary in South Carolina. Bill Clinton is not a racist, and I knew it could be a little lonely on the campaign trail. So, I called him. That's all."

Since then, I try to follow his advice. When friends are under the gun or feeling the heat for a comment that was taken the wrong way, I give them a call or send a quick text.

It is always appreciated. A little outreach goes a long way. And those little moments can come back to help you as well—it's part of building relationships and resources that can help you make sure that everything is okay for you, too.

Being a good friend rather than just a co-worker means showing up to things you might not want to go to or, if you're an introvert, that you might dread. The office birthday party or the anniversary lunch—things like that. Always make yourself go, and perhaps even help organize once in a while. Don't be a stick in the mud all the time. We need to show up for each other in life—otherwise, things can get pretty lonely.

Remember my rule: one drink maximum at work events (this includes the team building off-site that some companies do—like zip-lining or concerts). I know, talk about a stick in the mud! But this is a strongly recommended practice. It keeps you alert and fresh.

It prevents any problems or misunderstandings (or something even more serious). If you want to go out after the work party, great. Just don't have a big night out on the company's time or dime. As you observe the behavior of some co-workers who imbibe a bit more than they should, you'll see why this is a good practice. (A junior staffer in the early days of the Bush administration was out partying the night before he was to assist in an event at the White House. He overslept and came into the Oval Office crumpled and looking rough. The president noticed, gave him a subtle dressing-down, and believe me—the guy never again overindulged when work was bright and early the next day.)

You should look for opportunities to stick up for colleagues even when they aren't there—to share credit with them, to compliment them behind their backs. Do not look to be praised for this. Just do it when it's the right thing to do, and you'll gain a reputation for being a generous colleague. And that can pay dividends going forward.

Finally, make it a habit to brighten someone's day. Try doing it once a week. Can you send a note with a compliment for something that may seem out of the blue? What about writing a thank-you note to someone for being a great friend and colleague? Or calling unexpectedly to say how much you admire something they said or did in a meeting? You have to make this authentic—don't manufacture it (one rule: no poems). Look for ways to put a smile on someone's face. It really makes work more fun. And good deeds will come back to you one day as well.

REPEAT AFTER ME: NOT EVERYONE IS STUPID OR INCOMPETENT

Over the years, I've noticed that at any large organization, there are going to be a lot of things that go wrong, and you'll at some point think you know why it failed, that you have the magic wand that could solve it all.

I cringe when I hear junior employees suggesting that senior management at their workplace isn't smart (and this is from the broad swath of mentees that I work with across all sorts of industries). Look, management isn't easy. And they're in senior management for a reason—they've worked their way up. There could be a lot of factors that you just don't know about. And it's natural to commiserate with your colleagues. But you should avoid it—you can be dragged down and hurt by negative chitchat.

Bosses know when bad attitudes are creeping around an organization. They pick up on things and maybe even hear them through the grapevine.

And I've noticed patterns in some people who constantly harp on other people's management styles. This can be a fatal flaw. If you find yourself regularly thinking how you could do things so much better, pause for a second. Well, maybe you would. But if you express these thoughts all the time, you may end up holding yourself back and never get the chance to be a manager or get promoted.

Choose to be someone who doesn't pile on the negativity. Besides, one day you'll be running the joint, and then you'll see how it didn't serve you well as a young employee to assume you know better.

And when you think you know everything that's going on, ask yourself this: How much do others know about my life—truly know about my love life, family relationships, money situation, etc.? Chances are you'll realize how little you *really* know about what's driving the boss's decisions.

MANAGE UP TO MOVE UP

Handling the needs of a boss well enough to help achieve goals and get results is an undervalued skill. It's called "managing up." And if you're good at it, you'll get noticed. (Just be mindful that sometimes people who are managing up are considered to be getting the boss's attention at the expense of others—so manage that, as well. So much managing!)

What does it mean to manage up?

First, you have to understand your principal. Find the answers to these questions:

- What is the best time of day to approach them to answer questions you have? (Hint: it is probably *not* right before they have to present in front of the executive committee.)
- How do they like their day to be scheduled?
- Can you save them time by making appointments more efficient?
- What and *who* drives them crazy?
- Can you deftly handle rejections of requests for meetings or time on her schedule without offending the people asking?
- What is the best way to provide them information (paper, email, verbal briefing, smoke signals)?
- Do you need to get them a coffee and let them take off their coat and settle into the office before you start firing off requests that have come in?

If I do say so myself, I'm pretty good at managing up. It may have started with my experience waiting tables at restaurants. The customers are your boss—you have to get them what they ask for, anticipate their needs, check their orders, and hustle to prevent frustration and complaints. And make sure they leave happy and satisfied.

A lot of those skills I took to my work in Washington DC, first for the congressman and then for the president. Timing was really important—as elected leaders, they didn't have a lot of extra time on their hands. I learned to brief the president for an interview while we walked from the Oval Office to the East Wing.

"Not my first rodeo," he'd say.

"No, Mr. President, but you have to practice like you play!"

I would be efficient with my questions for him. I could get all I needed for the day's press briefing in the ten-minute flight from the South Lawn to Andrews Air Force Base. That made my briefing for the reporters on Air Force One go smoothly—no turbulence in the press cabin was one of my personal rules.

I'd also make sure that I had all my ducks in a row before I saw him every day. I imagined all the possible questions he might have for me. Then I'd work with my team to get the answers before I went into the Oval. Being respectful of his time ensured he'd want to see me again later. Anticipation and preparation are huge parts of any job—don't just wait to respond to emails from your boss. Get out of the back seat and into the front seat—prepare for the day so that you don't get run over by it.

One specific tip that I recommend is knowing how to deliver bad news to the boss in a way that is assuring, not alarming. This was actually one of the reasons my first book was called *And the Good News Is....* When I worked on Capitol Hill, my chief of staff told me she preferred to hear the bad news first. She said that's how the congressman liked to be informed, too. Sometimes, there's just no good news, so you have to come out and break it to them.

I suggest handling those situations (and why else do you go see the boss? It's not because you want to tell him, "The sun came up today, sir!") in this way:

"Everything is going to be okay, but we have an issue with [fill in the blank]." By leading with the assurance that it was going to be fine, you've diffused the tension and you've signaled that you already have a handle on whatever the problem is. This can shore up a shaky boss who has a big decision to make. Try this in your next interaction—and if you don't have some good news to leave on a high note, you can always say, "And the good news is we already have a jump on the next stage of this problem, so we are ahead of the curve and I'll provide you an update by the close of business on that." You will be pleased with their reaction. I promise this is definitely one way to show that you are ready for more responsibility.

Now, managing up also happens outside of politics and government. It happens everywhere. When I got into television after my White House years, I was very impressed with several producers who were pros at managing up. In their case, they're handling the concerns, questions, and anxiety of on-air talent, as well as the executives who want to make certain that the information going out to the audience is accurate, compelling, and entertaining. Everyone is under a lot of pressure, and keeping the hosts and anchors confident and assured is key to making good television.

During a presidential election cycle, the news business moves fast and travels a lot. There's a ton of information that we have to know. Being able to anticipate your boss's needs is critical. Once, during the 2020 cycle in New Hampshire, I remember looking up—at no one in particular—and saying, "I need…" but I couldn't find the words to what it was. My assistant, Hamdah Salhut, was standing there. She handed me what I needed. "This?" Yep, sure enough. Her attentiveness smoothed the way before we were live on air. (And no, it wasn't a shot of tequila.)

I only allow my assistants to work for me for two years. After that, they're kicked out of the nest and on to bigger and better things. I've loved them all and keep in touch with each of them.

Over time, my assistants all learned a lot about how to help me perform my work. (And you thought I was so easy! Ummm, didn't you?) For example, they know that I can't hold a retractable pen while I'm live on air because I have a nervous habit of clicking it, and that's picked up by the microphone, driving everyone in the control room *crazy*.

They know when to make sure I eat something and when to close the door so I can have a minute. They know when to send me a funny meme and when I need everyone to pay attention because I have something to say. Or when to send an alert that someone is coming down the hallway, or to whisper someone's name if they think I've forgotten it. They know what I need printed out and how I want a briefing formatted. These are just a few of the things I rely on them for. And their support has been invaluable and deeply appreciated.

One cold December day in 2018, I was part of the team at Fox attending and covering the funeral of President George H. W. Bush. It was an emotional time. I adored the forty-first president, and I would miss him. I felt for his family; they had just buried Mrs. Barbara Bush a few months before. It had been quite a year.

I'll never forget how Hamdah helped me keep everything together. She had this incredible tote, which I called her Mary Poppins bag. You wouldn't believe the things she had in there: an umbrella, protein bars, pens, highlighters, notebooks, and even a needle and thread that she used to help sew a button back onto Karl Rove's jacket just before the funeral. While he was in it! She made quite an impression. And that's what I mean about managing up.

Assistants are critical to an operation running smoothly, and they are way more valuable and powerful than their titles may suggest. If you're looking to hire someone, always consider someone who has been an assistant. They are entrusted with so much—they are required to handle a variety of situations while keeping their boss

even-keeled and able to do their job well. Good assistants can handle just about anything you throw at them—they can be your best
hires.

Now, part of working for someone is that you're a human and
something will go wrong at some point. Lots of somethings, actually. And sometimes it's not your fault. Maybe someone else dropped
the ball, or, more likely, your boss dropped the ball and might blame
you. What should you do then?

Let me give you an example. Not long ago I was asked to help
counsel a young woman who had upset her boss. The boss was frustrated because he'd missed an important conference call that was
being held on a weekend. The assistant had put the meeting on her
boss's calendar with two alerts to help make sure he didn't miss it.
She thought she'd done enough. She didn't email or text her boss
right before the call, thinking it was unnecessary (and truly, it could
have been—but it's always better to err on the side of caution, especially if it's something really important).

Anyway, her boss missed the meeting and was furious. He
looked irresponsible to his colleagues and he didn't get to weigh in
on an important matter up for consideration. He let her know he
was unhappy. Everyone felt miserable.

I talked to her. She was tempted to say, "It wasn't my fault." I
told her that response could make things worse. Then she told me
that she didn't even have her phone with her at the time because
it was her weekend and she "deserved some time off." Well. That's
undoubtedly true. Everyone deserves time off, yes. But when your
boss has an important call on a Sunday, would it really be too dis-
ruptive to your afternoon to send him a text to make sure he was
all set? Could taking thirty seconds to type out a message have prevented the problem in the first place? Do a cost-benefit analysis—the
cost of your boss missing the meeting is much larger than the cost of

the time it took to send him a quick text as a reminder. I call those little moments "ounces of prevention."

After my cost-benefit point was made, I suggested finding a good moment to knock on the door and ask for a few minutes. I recommended she say something along these lines: "I want to make sure that you never miss another meeting, so I'd like to confirm with you the way to do that. I put the reminder in your calendar and it should have popped up on your phone, though that wasn't as helpful to you as it could have been. What would be the best way to make sure this doesn't happen again?" (I told her to leave out the unspoken "you jerk.")

By doing this, she was trying to ensure that he'd see her calendar alerts, while also showing that she wanted to be proactive to guarantee smooth sailing going forward.

So much of managing up is in the approach: your tone, the timing, and the proposed solution. So, don't approach when your boss is super busy or about to be late for another meeting—you don't want to make it worse!

And remember an old saying: Sometimes the boss is right, sometimes not. But she's always the boss.

MANAGE YOURSELF FIRST

Managing people is really hard work. Most complaints from folks at the office are about how bad their manager is at their job. Everyone seems to think they know how to manage better; however, I recommend walking a mile in their shoes before trashing them too much. You might be surprised how difficult it is to be good at managing a team.

Before you become a manager, you first have to learn how to manage yourself. What does this mean? Think of it this way:

- Are you punctual? Do you arrive at work on time or do you often have an excuse as to why you're late? (Subway delays, traffic problems, volcanic eruptions—those can happen, but be honest about it.)

- Do you complete your tasks well, on time, and with no or few mistakes?
- Does your boss have to check on you often to see how you're progressing with a project, or do they leave you alone because they know you're going to finish it on time?
- Are you cheerful and friendly to others in the office and to clients and customers? Or could your personal vibe be described as "subarctic"?
- Do you bring a bad mood to your cube, or are you able to set aside personal concerns, or at least mask them, so that your negative energy doesn't affect others?
- In other words, are you a team player or a management problem? Because part of working for a good leader is being a good follower.

Try to avoid complaining about your manager with your co-workers—you never know what might get back to them, and it may be taken out of context and end up hurting your progress at the company without you even knowing it. Let's be honest—everyone loves *gossip*. But nobody likes *a* gossip.

If you manage yourself well, you're more likely to be tapped for promotion, and that usually means more responsibility...which includes managing other people. Until you can prove that you have your own house in order, the company will be hesitant to put you in charge of others. It's important to focus on this early on in your career, to create some good habits that you can carry with you through life.

And remember this: there is value in having lots of different types of managers, because it helps you shape your future approach to management.

There's as much to be learned from bad managers as there is from the good ones. We all have had experiences with bad bosses— be they bullies, lazy, incompetent, or mean. We can still conjure up memories of how they made us feel. How we wanted to quit and vowed we would never treat people like that. It might be worth writing down those negative qualities, too, so that you can remember what made you feel small and unappreciated. If you remember how that felt, you'll not allow it to happen to someone on your team.

But look, management is really tough. There's a reason why there are so many courses taught and books written on the topic. That's why it's a good idea to start planning for how you want to manage others now, so that you'll have a head start when you land that great new job you've had your eye on.

And in some sectors, women get a collective reputation for being poor managers with terrible temperaments (this is changing as more women climb the ladders and it isn't as unusual to have women in charge as it used to be). When I was taking over as the first Republican woman to be the press secretary at the White House, I picked up a great book that I still recommend: *The Girl's Guide to Being a Boss (Without Being a Bitch)*, by Caitlin Friedman and Kimberly Yorio. These two women ran a public relations company and they provide great suggestions for how you can be the best boss as a woman. Their experiences helped me think about how to manage my team in my own way.

Boiled down, my approach is to treat others how you'd want to be treated. (Pretty much everything in life comes down to that!)

I suggest picking a role model that you worked for and writing down what you liked about their style—how they motivated a team, handled problems, and got things done. How did they manage their schedule? What did they read? What was the best way to approach them with problems or complaints? How did they manage their bosses or the board? There's so much to be learned from observing a boss's behavior.

I often think about my first chief of staff, Holly Propst. She was a fantastic manager. Everyone wanted to perform well for her. We respected her so much. She would give clear direction, make sure we had the tools we needed to complete a task, and reward us with beers on Friday if everyone had their work done by that afternoon. We watched her handle tricky political situations, fully understand difficult policy issues, and manage the congressman we worked for with competence and efficiency. She was whip-smart and witty, as well as caring and approachable. So, when I'd face a problem, I'd think, *What would Holly do?* And then I'd try to solve the problem with my own version of those qualities.

I had really good managers to learn from at the White House as well. The best manager I've ever seen was President George W. Bush. Incredible instincts. He knew how to bring a team together and keep them inspired. President Bush surrounded himself with great people; in fact, in his book *Decision Points*, he writes about how the most important decisions he made when running the governor's office and the Oval Office were entirely about the people he hired. Personnel was paramount. Having hired the best people, he then empowered them to do their work. He didn't micromanage. He didn't have to. We wanted to perform well and we worked well as a team. He discouraged gossip and didn't let us snipe at each other. He always asked the best questions in every meeting to encourage a debate so that he got the best information, such as this question he asked during an economic policy time meeting: "Why is cutting tax rates on dividend income better policy than cutting capital gains taxes?" (A nerdy but important question!)

No one could out-read him (though Karl Rove tried!). They had a contest of how many books they could read in a year. Bush always won (and Karl didn't just let him).

President Bush could be demanding but had a light touch. He kept everything in perspective. He ran a very tight ship—his schedule was so packed, but he was almost always early to every meeting. He respected our time, so we respected his. I think that's the key to his management style—respect. We were stressed and under a lot of pressure, but we were also joyous. We laughed a lot—self-deprecating humor was appreciated. That was the perfect combination for me. I was motivated, dedicated, and enthusiastic about my work.

A big part of managing effectively is building loyalty between co-workers and between employees and executives. People work better if there is trust and a clear understanding that everyone is on the same team, working toward the same goal.

Let me further define what loyalty means to me.

It does not mean obeisance, where you have such deferential respect that you ignore or cover up faults or mistakes for someone else. It does not mean hiding the truth from them when they need to hear it. And it must never mean debasing yourself to help promote or protect them.

It does mean sticking up for someone when they're not around. Providing support and encouragement, even if a mistake was made and needs to be fixed. It can even mean being willing to take a punch for them.

Loyalty is about doing the right thing and being able to look yourself in the mirror and like what you see. And having that be its *own* reward. Because it might not even be noticed.

I remember one time on Marine One in the fall of 2008, right before the presidential election, when political advisors wanted to issue a statement by the press secretary about a court decision on gay marriage. They believed it would help some Republicans in tough races be able to take a stand that many supported at the time (that marriage was only between a man and a woman). We'd had this back-and-forth with the courts for years (ultimately the Supreme Court ended all of the legal wrangling when it ruled in favor of gay marriages in 2015).

I saw a message pop up on my phone. I read it and looked up at the senior staffer in charge of political outreach and shook my head.

President Bush never missed anything.

"What?" he asked.

I quickly gave him a summary of the court decision and the request for a statement (I learned to brief him clearly, quickly, and fairly so that everyone felt they had an even shot at getting the decision they wanted).

President Bush asked to see the proposed statement. I gave him my phone (thank goodness Peter hadn't just sent me some silly dog video right then). He put his reading glasses on and after a few seconds handed back my device, let his glasses slip to the tip of his nose, looked at the guys sitting next to me, and said, "She doesn't have to do that. Ever."

Then he looked at me and nodded.

And so, we didn't release a statement. His position on marriage had been clear for years. He knew it wasn't really going to make a difference in any of the races—it was a tough year for Republicans for a host of reasons, especially with the financial crisis. And he knew I didn't want to issue a statement against gay marriage in my name as the White House press secretary. We understood each other very well, and I have many other examples where I learned about loyalty by working with him.

The most important thing between a boss and an employee is respect. And sticking up for each other to build trust.

Remember that as you become a manager yourself.

Section #7: The big picture

Start to break away from the pack

PUT IT ALL TOGETHER

So—those are a lot of work tips and career advice. I could write these chapters twice as long, as there are so many issues we all deal with at work.

Does it feel overwhelming to think about incorporating this into your work life?

Remember my advice to break it up into bite-size chunks. I think that as an ambitious young woman, you could probably do more than that. But take it one step at a time if you need to. You're going to be working for many years—there is plenty of time to improve.

Is it worth taking an honest assessment of how you present yourself at work? How you might be perceived by your supervisors and your colleagues or the employees you manage?

Where can you make a few improvements to make your life easier, more pleasant, more productive? Are you being the best you at work?

Take these suggestions to heart and you'll see a difference.

Make a commitment; invest in yourself.

Don't get discouraged. Your path won't be a straight line.

And pass along these great tips to the next generation—they'll be working for you soon enough!

CHAPTER 6

⌁

How Do You Take Your Career to the Next Level?

When I found out I was being promoted to White House press secretary, I played it really cool with my team. When I was asked who I'd like to have for an assistant, I declined, saying I'd kept my own calendar for years and that I didn't think I'd need any help. Ha! Thankfully, they put a brilliant young man named Chris Byrne on my team, and I'd have been helpless without him. Chris got me where I needed to be, anticipated my requests, and kept me laughing. We've stayed good friends all these years.

Making that transition from staff to manager was a bigger learning curve than I anticipated. Not only was I managing a staff of fourteen, but I was also handling the senior staff, the cabinet, and the president regarding press office matters. It was *a lot*. I got through it, though I wish I'd had a book like this as a guide to making the shift smoother.

With the practical advice under your belt from the previous chapter, you're now in position to get more tips about progressing in your career. You've got one eye on the road and the other looking way ahead on the horizon, trying to make out what you see in the distance as your future. You'll get there. But you need to accept that you can't plan it all out.

There will be some twists and turns and a few detours. And when you arrive at your destination, it may not be what you envisioned when you were starting out. The good news is that the journey is not only fun and unpredictable, but it's part of what will help you achieve your goals.

After a couple of years—maybe more—of working, you will feel ready for more responsibility, a bigger role, and a chance to shine.

- How will you know when you're ready to move up?
- How do you figure out what your next step should be?
- How do you get others to see that you're the best choice for that job you really want?
- How do you set up your work and personal life to make the most out of your time?

This chapter will focus on answers to these questions, putting you on the road to future success.

It's time to lift your gaze from the daily tasks in front of you and see the career and life on your horizon.

This requires digging a little deeper, considering the inner traits that are important for success, and evaluating yourself on a scale beyond whether you can get through your daily to-do list. You're working to be a more resilient person, someone who is driven yet calm, super competent, and hopefully, cheerful through it all.

To go beyond the basics, start thinking about what is meaningful to you and how you will measure your satisfaction and success. What does that look and feel like when you picture it in your mind?

That's what we'll tackle in this chapter. I will provide some ideas for how to think about the bigger picture, and how to go from good to great and from just another employee to someone valued and indispensable.

I need you to commit to these three things to make this work:

- Make good personal choices. (As in, don't stay out until last call on a weeknight. And never leave on a motorcycle you didn't arrive on.)
- Take responsibility for your actions and outcomes. (Your dog has never eaten your homework—no one will ever buy that!)
- Start turning worry (that depletes you) into energy (that fuels you).

Let's get going.

Measure success

How do you measure success? I've given this a lot of thought.

As a kid, I loved the chart on the fridge that my parents used to give us red, blue, or gold stars for doing our chores and accomplishing school tasks. I craved affirmation. I wanted to get more than As on my report cards. I always did the extra credit. I always thought I could do better. I rarely took time to savor an accomplishment. Any recognition of good work made me want to work harder to get more praise. (I was an annoying child—*this is why Angie is the family favorite!*)

So how has that self-measurement manifested in me as an adult? Well, it makes me try harder, study more, and work smarter. It also pushes positive reinforcement. Getting a "Great segment!" from a producer or viewer after an interview will reenergize me. We all look for feedback like that. A little nudge that says, "You're on the right track." Even as grown-ups, we still want to put stars on our charts.

I know that I can be tough on myself. I always think I could have done better, pushed harder, or strived for more. It is an endless loop in my head. Part of that has given me an advantage, however, because I'm very driven and that's helped me succeed. And over time, I've figured out a balance where I can push myself to do well but not beat myself up for not doing everything perfectly. Give up perfection. But never give up *trying* for it. (Giving up on perfection is freeing for you, those you work with, and those you love.)

All of us measure ourselves differently, and how we rate ourselves depends on a lot of factors. Some people will define career success by how much money they earn, or whether they are promoted to a position at the top of their profession. Still others will measure it in terms of meeting a company's expectations or by how many employees they manage. The more important measure of success is personal satisfaction. And what you consider success can morph as your career changes and grows.

As my career took off, I got a lot of satisfaction from promotions I received. And I moved up pretty fast—in just a few years I went from being a spokesperson at the Justice Department to director of communications at the White House Council on Environmental Quality, to deputy press secretary, and then to the nation's spokesperson. There was a lot to be proud of. (Though there wasn't much time to reflect on it—I just had to keep my head above water!)

At the end of the White House years, I spent the last day with colleagues saying good-bye to President and Mrs. Bush. My favorite photograph is from the send-off at Andrews Air Force Base where President Bush caught my eye, reached over to cup my face in his hands, and planted a kiss on my forehead. That moment captured so much for me. And I think it was then that I felt like I'd accomplished something. As Peter and I drove to Dulles Airport to fly to the UK that afternoon, I leaned into the back seat of the car and said, "Nothing I do for the rest of my life will ever be that important or that hard."

My feeling of personal achievement didn't last that long, however. I started worrying pretty soon after that about what I'd be doing for work and how I'd earn a living. I was thinking about that before we got to the airport, in fact.

One way to measure your progress is, of course, financial security. And there's nothing wrong with that. I think about it. A lot.

Financial anxiety is a deep-seated worry of mine. When I was a teenager, I remember a moment when I decided I was going to be a financially independent woman. I never wanted to have to depend on someone else to pay my bills.

It took some time. When I graduated from college, my parents paid off the rest of my car, which was very generous of them. That took some pressure off me. When I worked on Capitol Hill, I could pay my bills, but there wasn't a lot to spare at the end of the month, especially with my student loan payment from graduate school.

Thank goodness for Desiree Sayle, my dear friend who let me rent her basement apartment. I basically ate with her family four nights a week at least. I checked out all the books I could possibly read from the Library of Congress, and my weekends included lots of "free" activities—city hikes, rollerblading, and biking. Those were tight but happy times.

There was a period when I moved to England to be with Peter when I didn't have a work visa. That was a good challenge for me during our early days together. I had to—and then relaxed into "got to"—rely on someone else to take care of me for a while.

When we moved back to the States, the roles reversed. Peter was starting a business, and then I was the one earning what we needed to cover our costs. Our shared experience helped us learn to trust each other and build a strong foundation for our marriage.

There is great freedom that comes from being in a strong financial position, and I recommend reading a good personal finance book, such as *Women & Money*, by Suze Orman (though there are several good books like this, I like her approach).

Invest in yourself by learning about the importance of not getting too deep into credit card debt, setting aside money every month for your savings, and taking advantage of offers for retirement accounts from your employer. Or, if you're a small-business owner or a freelancer, learn how you can help build your nest egg.

I know that one of my insecurities revolves around money and finances, and so having a reliable financial planner that we've worked with for twenty years has been helpful in alleviating that stress. He knew me when we were living paycheck to paycheck, and he's helped advise us along the way. Find someone you trust who can guide you on financial matters.

For me, given my anxiety about dealing with money, financial independence is one of the things I am most proud of. I clearly remember that moment when I committed to being able to take care of myself. And to realize I did it—that's really something. It means I am in charge, and it gives me a measure of control in that one aspect of life.

It also means that I am driven to step up every day and work hard to keep it.

And there's a reward in that work, too. A level of professional satisfaction that gets me to that feeling I crave the most—serenity.

There are other ways I measure myself—fitness and health, whether my jeans from last year still fit, if I've crossed off my home to-do list, if I remembered to call my mom. And I'm always thinking I could be a better wife, sister, daughter, friend, colleague, neighbor.

One of the ways to keep growing is to keep measuring ourselves. I think of my friend who just closed a twenty-year career heading up nonprofits in Colorado. Now she consults for a large philanthropic organization, helping them decide where their donations are needed the most. She has more personal time, so she joined a couple of community boards. She said it gives her so much fulfillment. The last time I saw her, she was glowing.

Maybe measuring ourselves shouldn't be so much about dollars and cents and titles, but about feelings. Can we take stock of our lives that way? That takes a leap of faith. We have conditioned ourselves to think we aren't succeeding if we aren't struggling. But I've seen a few friends let go of the struggle and then suddenly they're soaring. Maybe there's freedom and *more* success in letting go.

Can you get a gold star for *that*?!

Nothing is given; everything is earned

As you move up the ladder, your responsibilities are bigger and the stakes are higher. To be considered for another step up in your career, you have to prove you are competent.

How do you do that?

First, remember that you need to master the work in front of you before you take over another big job. Too many people want to skip over the early steps, expecting that the little things don't matter. Let me assure you—they matter. A lot. If you're not able to manage the basics of a job, if you cut corners, or if you blow off the details, you are in too much of a hurry and you won't be top of mind for new opportunities.

Second, be willing to take on the jobs that nobody else wants. The ones that aren't the coolest or where you get to have more face time with the boss. If there's an important function that needs to be done but isn't that exciting, raise your hand. Do that well, and I promise your competency will be noticed. This happened for me when I handled energy and environmental media relations at the White House.

At the same time, the nation was managing its response to the 9/11 terror attacks and working to keep the economy growing during all that uncertainty. Ari Fleischer, the press secretary, and Scott McClellan, one of his deputies, didn't have time to manage all the incoming media requests on environmental issues. I told them to send them my way. I took that off their plate. I answered questions on snowmobiles in our national parks, lawsuits against polluters, policy decisions on climate change, and even things like the Law of the Sea treaty. (Watch out for pirates!) I kept Ari and Scott informed of requests I got and let them know how I'd handled questions. I made sure that they had what they needed in case the national press corps came back on one of these issues.

So when the second term was about to get underway and Scott needed to replace one of his deputies who was going to work at the Commerce Department, he knew that I was able to handle tough issues without a lot of fuss. He asked me if I'd be interested in the job. Was I interested? I was thrilled—and grateful that I'd spent those years digging in to really understand energy and environmental issues. To this day, I gravitate to those stories in the newspaper.

My point is to do the nonsexy job as well as you can, so that you'll be top of mind when the sexy job opens up. Don't wait to prove your competence when you're applying for a new job. Let your work precede you.

I also suggest keeping track of your accomplishments, so that you don't have to reinvent the wheel each time you are asked for examples of your work product. This is a good practice for your reviews, too. Think of it as an accomplishment diary. You might forget something along the way, so it's a good practice to have it written down.

One way to do this is to create an email folder that you can put messages in that you'll want to call upon later. For example, a congratulatory note from your supervisor or a client for a job well done, articles that mention your team's success on a project, and thank-you messages from employees you've helped.

Competency is the key to more responsibility and future success, and being able to *show* competency is up to you. Having these materials at your fingertips will save you time and prevent you from forgetting something that may really help you make your case for a promotion, raise, or a new client. It also shows you can keep many balls in the air at once—the key to being seen as leadership material.

Paying your dues

With competency comes compensation. You get paid for your work.

Secretary Rice says that many of her students at Stanford tell her that they want to do something meaningful in their work. She says that sure, everyone wants that. But when you're starting out, you will do the work that they ask you to do. And the meaningful part is that you'll get a paycheck for the work that you do.

The issue of pay is always on the minds of workers. Getting paid fairly and, hopefully, well is important.

There is more transparency and fairness in compensation at more of today's companies than in the past. There is also more information online about average salaries in various fields, so that you can have an idea of what to expect to be paid for positions that you may want.

In government, there were pay scales that I fell under, so I didn't have a lot of leeway to earn more unless I moved up a level. Then when I had my own business, I had to calculate how much I should get paid for consulting work based on how much time I'd spend on the project and how intense or difficult the endeavor was. When I moved into television, I worked with a lawyer who helped negotiate my compensation. For me, that was a good way to handle discussions of pay. I am not that comfortable talking about money. (Peter is much better at it, so I rely on him for that, too!)

To get you the best advice, I went to Lydia Fenet, managing director and global head of strategic partnerships at Christie's and author of a must-read book, *The Most Powerful Woman in the Room Is You: Command an Audience and Sell Your Way to Success.*

Lydia told me she didn't grow up being super comfortable talking about money. But knowing that she wanted to make more of it, she got over her anxiety and now is willing to share her tips with others.

First, she says that you have to be your own advocate.

"If you don't know how to promote yourself, nobody will do it for you. Women think they shouldn't promote themselves, but they absolutely must. You can take control of that and be in charge," she said.

One of her best stories is when she found out that a good friend was buying an apartment in Manhattan. She was floored. She couldn't see how it was possible that one of her peers was in a position to actually buy an apartment. She thought they were all making about the same amount of money. Turns out they weren't. And that's when Lydia decided she had to make some changes.

"Women never talk about money—but they need to. How do you know what you should be paid? You need to ask friends, even if that is uncomfortable. Be candid and be willing to share," she said. "A lot of guys do that all the time—they literally compete over how much money they're making. It's like sport for them. Women don't like to do it, but knowing what people are being paid means more clarity for your own negotiations."

Lydia said salary comparison sites are okay but that conversations are better. And that if you're not comfortable asking direct questions, reach out to a friend to help find out for you. She said this is important because you need to have a benchmark for your salary.

How often should you ask for a raise? "Every year," she said. "The best way to get the kind of salary you want is to be very transparent with your boss. Get them to help you lay out a plan that includes how much money you want to make and how you're going to get there. Have this conversation early on."

And if you don't get a raise every year, should you look for another job?

She said that if you're not getting promoted or more money every year, you should be realistic (actually, she said don't be *ridiculous*) and help yourself by coming up with a plan.

But how do you even start the conversation, especially if you've been at a company for a while?

"It's never too late to have the conversations. If your boss doesn't know what you want, she might think you're just happy."

And her final words of advice: You are what you negotiate. You can't think something is unfair if you never even ask.

I can do it! (I think . . .)

I'm going to take a wild guess and say that on any given day, you have a lack of confidence in your abilities at work.

How do I know I'm right? Because I feel that way every day, too! It's usually not a crushing lack of confidence for me, but I sometimes have to give myself a little pep talk.

"I've got this!" is something you need to start telling yourself. Even if you have doubts, talk yourself up a bit.

I believe deep down that all of us are unsure of things throughout the day—some of us power through and hide it well while others worry openly about whether they can complete a task. Again, here, I think there's room for some balance.

When you're part of a team, or the manager of a group, you have to have some confidence that you'll make good decisions. Otherwise, no one will follow you. This doesn't mean having all the answers at the beginning of a project. But it means knowing the general direction you want to go and the basic things that need to happen to get to the finish line. It means being flexible as obstacles present themselves, not panicking when something goes wrong. Can you be the "steady as she goes" leader in the office? You bet you can. And once you've done it a few times, you'll see that people will look to you to help solve problems. And then brick by brick, you build a stronger and stronger foundation of confidence.

I remember gaining in confidence when I was the deputy press secretary and Tony Snow would delegate the morning senior staff meeting to me. The press and legislative affairs offices went first. We kicked it off with our needs—answers to questions from reporters and members of Congress. We teased out problems and conflicts and set the tone for the day.

I had a knack for spotting trouble ahead—often because my team and I read everything we could to make sure we had our bases covered. I noticed that the senior staff was listening to me. They thought what I had to say was worth hearing and didn't just think of me as a junior staffer but as someone who had an important role.

It was empowering and helped build my confidence. The more confident I felt, the more people came to me for advice. And as I started to become a leader, I was less hesitant to make decisions. I trusted my instincts. I was not shy about giving my opinion. And I noticed that I was being given even more responsibility. Soon enough I was the press secretary, after Tony decided for health reasons that he needed to step down. I don't think I realized at the time that he had so much confidence in me that he felt he could leave senior staff to me. He also had me brief the president for interviews and press conferences. He asked me to manage the office staff. Not only was Tony a great boss for allowing me to handle those tasks, but he was helping me realize what he saw in me. I'll always be grateful for that, and I try to do the same with my colleagues now. Empower someone, trust them, help them up when they stumble—there's great satisfaction in that, and it can help you make sure great work is being done without you having to micromanage.

There are times when I've had a crisis of confidence, wondering whether I'd said the wrong thing or made the wrong call. I am fortunate to have Peter and a good circle of friends to talk things over with. When you're making tough calls or taking a risk, you can tie yourself up in knots if you spend a lot of time second-guessing yourself. To keep a healthy level of confidence, if you are worried a decision wasn't the right one, just be prepared to change course. Be flexible (and human!).

Once in a while, you'll find that someone you work with has a real lack of confidence, despite all evidence pointing to how well they are doing and how highly they are regarded. Being underconfident can be worse than being overconfident because it holds you back.

Now, there are modest people, and that humility is certainly welcome at times. But I'm talking about the people who are doing so well and yet they still think that they're not ready, not good enough, not smart enough, etc. They get into a negative, self-denying vortex. And it's important to help coach them along so that they can be productive and help you achieve your goals. Take time to shore them up, because if they can be more confident in the tasks you've put them in charge of, then you can focus your energy on whatever other problems are in front of you.

And if you yourself are reading this and thinking, *Oh boy, I could be the kind of person Dana is talking about*, are you undercutting your progress because you're so modest, or are you so worried that you're not measuring up that you're missing out on promotions and opportunities? Do you constantly put yourself down, even when your manager is praising you? Is your reticence to embrace your confidence holding you back?

If the answer to any of these is yes, then you have to (a) snap out of it and (b) start to work on it.

There are a lot of tools out there to give you a boost. Podcasts like *She Said / She Said, WSJ's Secrets of Wealthy Women, WorkLife,* and *I Want Her Job* are so interesting. I always learn something. I also recommend books like the aforementioned *The Most Powerful Woman in the Room Is You* by Lydia Fenet and a classic, *How to Win Friends and Influence People.*

Building confidence takes time. If you feel a little less than sure of yourself, understand that's normal, but don't let it take hold of you. Reach down deep and be honest with yourself on this point—you can pull yourself through. Think of how many things you've gotten *right*—and draw strength from that.

And confidence is attractive. As you feel more confident, you'll start to feel a little taller, raise your gaze a little higher (posture!), and maybe even the corners of your mouth can lift into a smile. Confidence builds on itself. Start to lay a strong foundation that will serve you well for the rest of your life.

Getting out of your own way

What if the obstacles on your career path have been put there by you—and you don't even realize it?

There are a lot of ways this can happen. For example, as I just described, having a lack of confidence can hold you back. Another way is to be so worried about what other people are thinking about you, and wanting to be liked.

Look, I want to be liked, too. In fact, a few years ago I was really bothered by some social media comments regarding my commentary on a political issue. I really agonized over it. I wanted to fix it, but of course, trying to fix social media is a fool's errand.

During that time, I was asked at a speech what it was like to be someone with an unpopular opinion. I said, "Well, I used to think I was America's sweetheart. Now they look at me as America's ex-girlfriend."

I was perhaps overly harsh in my self-criticism, and I tried to make light of it. But it really was tough to go through the backlash.

I didn't know until a year later that most of the online criticism that was fired at me was coming from bots and trolls who were programmed and paid to make me and others feel like crap. They wanted people like me to get so fed up or upset that we'd be cowed into silence. I was surprised how affected I was by what these accounts were saying to and about me online. On any given day, social media is a time and energy suck—but when it starts to affect how you feel about yourself, making you miserable, it is definitely time to stop engaging. (Once the social media companies purged the fake accounts, nearly all of the vitriol went away. It was a fascinating lesson to learn.)

Around that time, I asked a friend, Adam Grant, an organizational psychologist, about what I was feeling, and he suggested a book I really liked called *Women Who Think Too Much*, by Susan Nolen-Hoeksema. My main takeaway from that was that I had a tendency to think too much about things that didn't matter, like what other people were thinking of me. The good news is they most likely weren't thinking about me at all. People are naturally very self-centered. We are always thinking about ourselves—it's part of our survival instinct. But it can become a problem when we obsess about what others are thinking of us.

This reminder allows you to let go of that worry of what others are thinking about you because chances are, they're not. (An exception is when the cyberbullying or cyberstalking crosses a line into possible danger to you or others—if that ever happens, report it to your supervisor and company security or to law enforcement authorities. You are not alone in experiencing this, and don't hesitate to address it to stay safe. Trust me—it won't be the first time they've heard it.)

The good crowd

Now that you are getting out of your own way, you have to figure out how to get negative people out of your way. You know the people I mean—the ones who drag you down with their negative energy and their gossip about co-workers that makes you uncomfortable and who bad-mouth the boss a little too loudly. We've all been there.

Let me ask you—if you had shoes that always gave you a blister and never got broken in, would you keep wearing them? No. You'd get rid of them or push them to the back of the closet because even though they're adorable and they cost a lot of money, the agony isn't worth it.

I like to work with people on solving problems. I just don't like to do it with someone who is dragging the team down. There are some people who wallow in misery, and since misery loves company, they try to recruit more people to complain with them so that they can justify their feelings. You might be tempted to respond, just to keep the peace. But it can be unproductive, even hurtful, to your career if you do.

A friend of mine works in the finance sector and got burned when she tried to help a Negative Nellie who was having a hard time with her boss. My friend offered to share some of the workload to make it easier on her colleague. Welp. Instead of being gracious, the woman started looping my friend into her problems and then started blaming her for them! She said it was a hard lesson to learn—she tried to help but ended up being dragged down by her colleague.

"There's a difference between helping and getting involved in the drama or helping them by completely removing yourself," she said. And she recommends a book called *The No Asshole Rule* by Robert I. Sutton that can help anyone dealing with a situation like this. (Also, it's a cool title and a great rule!)

If you've fallen in with the wrong crowd, but you didn't realize it until it felt like it was too late, start to extricate yourself from the situation. Slowly back away. This is true for your workplace, your friends, and even sometimes your family.

Or maybe someone in your circle of friends has changed over time, or you've changed; regardless, if that friendship isn't serving you well, distance yourself from that person. You can remain friendly. You don't have to cut anyone off completely (unless it's truly toxic and that would serve you well). But if a person is not adding something positive to your life, find a way to remove them from your path.

Here's a term: "negative energy." Who came to your mind first? Should you be reassessing your relationship with that person? (Hopefully it's not a loved one. At least we know it'll never be your dog.)

You have goals to achieve, so don't let yourself be held back by others because you feel bad or worry about what they'll think of you. Remember, people, by and large, think only about themselves. You'll be doing yourself, your family, and your career a service by cutting off any negativity in your life.

Your circle of friends... lean on them

As you remove negative people from your life, you should be adding positive people to your circle of friends and colleagues. This is also called your network. I've been so supported over the years by the people I've worked with along the way. This includes my college roommate, Andrea Aragon, as well as several people I met on Capitol Hill, within the Bush administration, in my public relations business, and now at Fox News. Not a day goes by that I'm not in touch with many of them, and usually it is because we are talking about what we love best—politics and news of the day. They help me think things through, suggest points that I could make, and remind me of historical examples I can sprinkle into my commentary.

And we are there for each other through the ups and downs, including the joy of a newborn child, the worry when parents are in ill health, and the big moves across the country—for one friend, that's been six times now! (She steps out on her rent. Just kidding.)

We help each other when we're in a position for a new job opportunity or promotion, when we are hiring and looking for good people to join our company, and when we are weighing any big life decisions—such as a career change or dealing with raising teenagers in the modern world.

And we show up for each other—the parties, events, the moments that mark achievements and celebrations. This circle of friends has helped me more than I can say, and it has been the key to my life's enjoyment. Invest in your friends. Help them; lean on them. And they'll be there for you, too.

How can you build a network like this? Think of it as a board of personal advisors. A board is made up of people from different walks of life, different experiences that help give perspective that you may not have. And a board keeps people accountable, making sure you're working on reaching your goals.

If I were starting out in my career today, I think I'd try to find the following type of people to be on my board: a cultural expert, a historian, an academic or intellectual on politics and demographics, a foreign policy guru, an artist, a psychologist, and a comedian (you gotta laugh!). Oh, and a lawyer. Just in case.

This board would meet three times a year—like a girls' weekend with manicures, margaritas, and mentoring. But they'd be people I'd keep in touch with and get to know so that I can help them in times of need and be able to ask their views on matters important to me.

Start to build your board. You don't have to extend a formal invitation, unless you really want to get serious. I suggest making friends with these people, learning about them, and keeping a schedule to be in touch. You might let them know what your goals are and see what they think. Bounce some ideas off them. They'll be as invested in your success as you are in theirs.

My advice is to do something that keeps this circle intact. We have the tools to stay in contact quite easily. It doesn't take much. And you'll be rewarded for it over and over.

Here are a couple of networking tips, updated for our social media world. It used to be that you'd have an address book that was written out, with some friends' information scratched out over and over as they moved, got married, and moved again. I used to take my address book and then randomly choose five people a week to send postcards to. I'd start in the *A*s and work my way through the alphabet. When I was done, I'd start all over. On the cards, I'd just write a little update about myself and inquire about their lives, wishing them well. Simple, quick.

Now you can network in all sorts of ways using social media, and it's way more efficient and effective. A friend of mine who works for Big Tech has developed a natural habit of networking. She follows her colleagues and keeps in touch with friends and former employers at previous jobs. Every time she meets someone, if they are a person she wants to know, she'll follow them on LinkedIn, Instagram, or Facebook. If someone posts a neat photo, she'll comment with a compliment. If another is quoted in an article, she'll cut and paste the quote and send an email or a message on LinkedIn, with a note about how the quote was smart or how it spoke to her that day. She isn't sending a note with a specific request or need—she's just keeping in touch. She said that inevitably she'll get a response and there will be a brief exchange, often including "What are you up to these days?" That's a great way to keep in touch with a lot of people in an efficient way, and it ensures that you're on their radar in case opportunities come their way that they think you'd be perfect for.

I keep a list in my Notes app of people I want to connect with—then at least once a week, I'll set aside some time to send a note, a direct message, or a text that says, "It was great to catch up," or, "I saw your company is expanding and I hope that means great things for you."

I also reach out when things might not be going so well, or when someone is under fire for expressing an opinion that stirs up a hornet's nest (the hornets never rest in journalism these days).

Here's an example: Leading up to the 2020 election, I sent an old friend a note about a column she posted about what she thought was likely to happen on Election Day. I said, "Thanks for helping me think this through."

She responded that it was a relief to see my email—it was the only nice one in a pile of angry notes she was getting from both sides. It didn't take a lot for me to know she'd be under fire and that, instead of piling on, I could just reach out and encourage her. I believe she'll do the same for me when I inevitably need some shoring up in the future. I call it mutually assured construction.

And that helps you have a ready-made set of connections in case you are ready to start looking for a new job, need advice about a career change, or unexpectedly find yourself in need of employment because of a layoff or furlough. Having a network helps you position yourself to have people to call to help you get through it. That's one of the ways you make sure everything will be okay.

Your network is *power*—a force multiplier for you. And women tend to be natural networkers. So get to work on yours. It will pay long-term dividends.

The having-it-all trap

Moms are amazing people. They already have the most important job of helping raise little babies to be good, productive people. And many of them are working as well. Managing a career and raising children is something I'm quite in awe of.

Since I don't have children myself, I turned to my friend Michele Chase (aka Superwoman!) to help give you some of her best advice on "doing it all."

Michele has been in human resources for over twenty years. During that time, she rose to the top of her field as global chief talent officer.

She's also an incredible wife, mother, sister, and friend. She's one of my "I don't know how she does it" friends.

Michele and her husband, Tim, were the parents of two boys, living in New York City, and had found a way to make it all work.

She had just been promoted to the global head of human resources at her company, so she was feeling pretty good about how things were going.

What she didn't know was that she was also pregnant. Surprise! (One of my favorite stories is how she threw a pregnancy test at her husband, Tim, when he came in from a fun day of watching the Jets play and she'd stayed home taking care of the kids and making his favorite chili.)

"What?!" Tim asked. When he saw what it was, he said, "This can't be right."

Oh … it was right!

Michele told me she wouldn't have accepted the big promotion if she had known she was going to have a third child. I was surprised because I've seen her handle it all with such grace.

"These are the kinds of limitations women put on themselves," she said.

She had to make a decision—should she keep the new job?

"I thought, *How am I going to do this?* And the answer was, *Well, I'm just going to do it!*" she said.

Colleagues wondered how she would handle the load, too. In response, she asked them, "That's funny. I bet nobody's asking my husband how he's going to handle everything when the third baby arrives."

"Life happens. You take it as it comes. You just have to do it," she told me.

Lesson: We Put Up Our Own Restrictions, Building Barriers Around Ourselves. And Let Go Of Feeling Guilty About Working. Dads Don't Feel Guilty About Working—They're Expected To Work.

Michele also said that being firm in saying no, thereby setting boundaries, is very important. Her goal was to have dinner with her family most nights. And everyone in the office knew it. She says it is very important to communicate your needs because people aren't psychic—they don't know what you have going on in your life. You don't have to go into a ton of detail. But saying you need 6:00 to 8:00 p.m. free from work emails or meetings will give people a way to work around that.

Lesson: Let People Know What You Need To Manage Work And Family. If You Don't Tell Them, You Can't Get Angry With Them For Not Understanding.

One way Michele reinforced this was if someone did call her during her designated family time, and if the kids were crying or fighting in the background, she would just pick up the phone and ask how she could help them. Hearing the natural chaos of a home with young children would have the effect of them apologizing for the interruption—they knew she'd be back on email after the kids were in bed. Whatever they were calling about could wait. It never seemed to be an emergency.

Lesson: Never Apologize For Having Kids.

The decision to go back to work or stay at home is very personal and neither choice is wrong. Michele says that if you decide to take an extended time to raise your young children, it's critical to keep your foot in the work world somehow if you plan to go back in the future. That can include consulting or freelancing.

"The world changes while you're at home. It's like driving a car off the lot—as soon as you do, the car loses value," she said. The longer you stay out of the workforce, the harder it is to get back in.

New technology is created, new people arrive, programs and policies change.

"I wanted to go back to work like my rear end was on fire. I knew I needed to get back to where I could eat my lunch and not worry about anyone sticking their finger in a socket! Though if you don't go back to work after having a child, stay in touch and maintain those work relationships and friendships. You never know if or when you will want to return, but those people are the ones who know and will remember how it was to work with you after you've been out of the workforce for a few years."

Lesson: Take The Time You Need To Raise Your Children And Set Them Up For Success. But Do Not Neglect Your Work Life For Long—Stay On Top Of It So That You Can Maintain The Skills You Need And Hold The Salary You Earned Before You Had Kids.

Michele describes her life as packing twenty-eight-hour days into twenty-four hours. One way she did that was to wake at 5:00 a.m. so that she could have an hour to herself when no one else was awake. "That's my time," she said.

She keeps this thought in mind: "I only have them for eighteen years. I tell myself, at a certain point my house will be clean. Until then, I don't want to miss any of these moments."

She makes the most of that time. As her boys got a little older, she had a bit more time and could pursue a new passion—painting. "It makes me feel good when I do it," she said.

Lesson: You Are A Whole Person, Not Just A Piece. Taking Care Of Yourself, Attending To Your Needs, Gives You The Ability To Be 110 Percent At The Office And 110 Percent At Home. Just Remember That Nothing Needs To Be Perfect And Having Different Parts Of Your Life Left In A "Comfortable State Of Undone-Ness" Is Totally Okay And Necessary.

Mistakes have been made

I'm the kind of person that can really beat myself up for mistakes, particularly at work. I have a hard time shrugging things off when it is something I've done, but I'm quick to forgive others. Go figure!

I can still call up mistakes I made even when I was waiting tables in college (dumping a tray full of mimosas on a gentleman's white pants during Father's Day brunch—he was so nice about it, though)... when I was a country music deejay (announcing that we were about to play "her" new song—Tracy Lawrence... of course, after the first few bars when the vocals began, I realized that Tracy is a man)... when I gave a quote to *Roll Call* about then Speaker Newt Gingrich's decision on some piece of legislation and didn't run it by my boss the congressman beforehand (ugh—that one still stings!)... when I didn't raise my voice loudly enough at the White House to prevent a negative news cycle from bubbling up regarding a foreign investment story about Dubai Ports World...and then there are all the times I've messed up on live television. Nothing catastrophic, thankfully. But enough to still make my cheeks turn red.

One example was during the last segment of *The Five* where each co-hosts gets to bring up something funny or interesting that they've seen, and my colleague put up a video of a Florida man holding a small alligator, tape around its mouth, going into a convenience store and scaring everyone by putting it right in their faces. The customers were screaming—they were so scared!

I was horrified. I would have been terrified if I'd been one of those people. I probably would have kicked him right where it counts.

As we watched the video, I said, "What an *asshole*!"

Well, that's a no-no. And it was so unexpected coming from me that the table erupted into laughter and couldn't recover. My stomach burned as I worried about the consequences of my actions—I just *hate* to get in trouble. I had lost my composure and said the quiet part out loud. I can still feel the embarrassment.

Thankfully, it turned into something funny. And even the president of Fox News got a call from his mom imploring him not to get mad at me, because it was just a mistake, and, "Besides, she was right!" Truth is a defense, after all.

It's a strange thing how humans are wired to remember negative things rather than positive ones. I know that you can recall easily when you got a bad review or someone said something you did was poorly done. I bet you can remember every detail of where you were, what you were wearing, and whether it was sunny or rainy when you got that negative feedback or when you made a mistake. But can you think of an example when you were praised, thanked, or appreciated? Rarely. It is just the way we are.

Please try to find a way to be nicer to yourself. Can you let a mistake go? Maybe laughing about it is the best way. Mistakes aren't usually funny at the time, but they make for great stories later.

One of my favorite stories is about Peter's early career as a salesman. He was in Scotland working for an auto parts company. One day he had to make a visit to Big Jimmy who lived way up in the Highlands. It was a cold day, and Peter was chatting to Jimmy while Jimmy was repainting a car. Peter recalls rubbing his hands together and stamping his feet to try to get warm. Unfortunately, he accidentally kicked over an oil heater and the ashes rose into the air and then settled all over the freshly painted car. Well, Big Jimmy picked Peter up by the back of his jacket and the seat of his pants and threw him out of the garage. As he landed, Peter felt his briefcase hit him in the head. (He wasn't called "Big Jimmy" for nothing.)

"And don't effing come back!" Big Jimmy yelled.

Peter scurried away, agonized about what happened.

A few months later, Peter's boss said that Big Jimmy had called and wondered why he hadn't had a visit in a while, because he needed to place an order. Peter finally told him what happened, and with time they were able to have a good laugh about it.

Peter eventually went back to see Big Jimmy. There were no hard feelings.

Learning from your mistakes and letting go of them is the key to becoming more resilient in life.

You have the power not to let mistakes or errors turn into something bigger than they are. Don't let something that happened once hold you back from future success. To do that would be a huge... er... mistake.

But hey—everyone makes mistakes. A lot of them. As we get older, at least at the office, we make fewer of them (but they do tend to be more important). But it still happens to all of us. We all need to learn from our mistakes and move on. And if you're a manager, you have to set the example of moving on. Never dwell on someone's mistake, especially if it really wasn't that big of a deal. Never rub their noses in it. That's a terrible way to manage a person. If you handle it well, you'll make sure that you have their loyalty and that they'll never do something like that again.

A final lesson here: look forward, not backward. Because you can control your reactions to things in the future, to some extent. But you can do nothing about the past. Realize that and you'll be much more successful.

Letting go of letdowns

To me, disappointment is one of the toughest emotions to manage. It just stinks. I don't like to be disappointed, and I really dislike disappointing others. I don't even like to *think* about being disappointed.

Letdowns, however, happen in life:

- Losing a big game in overtime
- Not getting to travel for a big work meeting
- Being turned down for a promotion or a job
- Losing out on an opportunity to buy your first house
- Breaking up with someone who turned out to be a dud (trust me—you'll thank yourself later)

Disappointment will happen, but how you manage being disappointed is important to your well-being and to building your resilience.

Some people bounce back from disappointment very well. "There's always next year!" or "That was an amazing game!" Others take a more philosophical approach: "Maybe this is for the best." Still others see it as an opportunity to try again. I admire these people. My husband, Peter, is one of them. He can take a disappointment, think on it for a while, and be very measured in his handling of it.

While I believe in positive thinking, I am a little more pragmatic and know that the outcomes I want aren't always going to turn out in my favor.

One of the ways I cope is trying to balance my hope for how something will turn out with how I will feel if it doesn't work out. I plan for the best and prepare for the worst. That works for me, so that I can visualize and "emotionalize" that I'll be fine whatever the outcome.

I did that in 2004 during the reelection campaign of President Bush. Polls had the president way down in the summer. My mom called, worried that I was going to be unemployed. I said we'd all lose our jobs and that it was normal in DC. Not to worry.

A few days later she called back and said, "You're so good at your job maybe John Kerry would want to keep you." I told her it doesn't work that way, but thanks for the vote of confidence!

Her call got me thinking about how I'd manage the disappointment if President Bush lost the election. Of course, he won and I kept my job, but I was ready for the just-in-case scenario.

Another way I prepare myself for disappointment is to pray. I don't pray for specific outcomes like, "Please, Lord, let those shoes be in stock in my size." God is way too busy for that. Instead, I pray that God will help me be wise in how I handle how something turns out. This approach has helped me maintain serenity in times of sadness or disappointment.

Prepare yourself with a strong and flexible mindset to help deal with disappointments. You don't want to freak out or be devastated—build up some resiliency. Hope for the best, prepare for the worst, and remember that the race is long.

Let me tell you about a friend who was recruited within her company to be promoted into a new role managing communications. She was told by the executive doing the hiring that she was "the best for the job" and very talented, with a great reputation, etc. In fact, he said she was so good at her job that she might even butt heads with him and be stronger than he was in the role. That didn't deter her. She wanted the promotion and prepared all weekend for the challenge. She bought two suits and planned her first moves in the new role.

However, come Monday, she was told she wasn't getting the job after all. The executive team decided to go with a different candidate (weaker in qualifications than my friend). She was very disappointed and didn't know what had happened. And she never got a good answer as to why she was passed over for someone else.

But it turns out she dodged a bullet. The man that was hired instead of her was miserable in the job. He had no autonomy, no authority, and no initiatives—nothing entrepreneurial at all.

So, it all worked out in the end—not getting the job actually enhanced her reputation at the company. She was seen as above that role and ultimately ended up with an even bigger job.

Remember—disappointments will happen. And you learn from those experiences. Trust me that there will always be other opportunities, even if you don't see that now.

Channeling the stress and worry into something positive (and low calorie)

Stress is the worst—especially if you let it get the best of you. Without actively managing stress, you'll not perform as well at work, you might bite the head off a loved one for no good reason, and you could end up losing sleep or gaining weight. In the extreme, stress that isn't managed can cause illness and depression.

Everyone has stress in their lives—job pressure, money problems, child rearing, dating woes, aging parents. It comes in lots of different ways.

Some people don't really feel alive if they aren't stressed. They feed off drama. Others share their stress with their colleagues, trying to make sure that the stress is spread out (not cool, dude).

Here's the deal—since there's no getting around being stressed, you have to find ways that help you deal with it.

I have a few things that have helped me.

First, exercise is key. I remember Condoleezza Rice talking about the need for humans to exercise because it's the only way we're able to work off stress so that we can think more clearly.

I really identified with that. I love all sorts of exercise (except running! I don't even run errands if I can help it). I try to exercise in some way every single day—from riding my indoor bike to Pilates, to weight training, to yoga. And don't forget the posture videos!

I know friends who knit to relieve anxiety, and others who practice meditation. I find it hard to sit still for that long when I have so much to do. (This is why I actually need to meditate!)

Sleep is a good way to relieve stress, too. Falling asleep can be tough if you have a lot on your mind, so I recommend a guided sleep meditation from an app like Headspace or Calm to help you get your Zzzz's. Practicing good sleep habits is important. There are a lot of articles out there on this topic that explain the importance of sleep and how to get more of it (and better quality). Tips include turning off your phone an hour before bed, having a set bedtime and sticking to that routine, and avoiding caffeine after 4:00 p.m. (though some even say no coffee after noon—that seems impossible for many, I know).

During the COVID-19 pandemic, athletes who were meant to

compete in the Olympics instead found themselves with a lot more time to train and work out, as well as sleep. Several of them ended the lockdown faster and stronger than before. They were breaking their own records. And all of them said that getting more sleep was the key. So: train for your career like an athlete does for competitions!

Another way to deal with stress and get better sleep is to write down what's bothering you. Putting the worries on paper turns them into problems that can be solved, rather than thoughts that loop in your head.

Sometimes I ask Peter to look at my list, and he'll help talk things through so that I can let stress go. One of my favorite examples is when I called him full of tears because I'd been kicked out of the Oval Office.

I was caught up in a miscommunication between the president and the communications director over an interview with a columnist—I was an innocent bystander, but when the president gave his final answer that he was not going to do the interview, he looked my way and said, "Therefore, she doesn't need to be here." He cocked his head to signal I was dismissed.

I backed out and tried to hold it together as I walked the fifty feet back to my office. Once there, I closed the pocket door behind me and called Peter.

"What's wrong?" he said.

My voice was quiet and shaky. I blinked back tears and told him what happened.

"Well, just think. For the rest of your life you can say, 'I've been kicked out of better places than this!'" he said, making me laugh.

Of all the things that I do to deal with stress, I think laughing is the most effective. I try to see the funny side of things, to lighten a mood.

It's important to build some stress management skills so that you won't feel burned out. People who are stressed out are not fun to work with, and they can be a drag on a team. And there's your family's well-being to consider—don't bring the stress into the house. Find a way to leave it at the door.

Unfortunately, there's no magic pill, drink, or substance that is going to alleviate your stress (without possibly causing other problems).

Use your stress to channel energy into your work. Take that worry and turn it into action—that can include exercising, writing in a journal to clear your thoughts, or getting ahead in reading before you start work on Monday. Think of it this way: stress is energy that you can utilize to be more successful. Make it work *for* you instead of against you.

Time is on your side (yes it is)

Part of stress management is time management.

I've tried to stop answering the simple question "How are you?" with "I'm so busy!" Everyone is busy. How we manage our busy is up to us.

There isn't much white space in my calendar. I hit the ground running, reading the news and preparing for the day's shows very early in the morning. I speed read, thankfully. After a couple of hours of reading and listening to the important podcasts of the morning, I always take one hour, usually from 8:00 to 9:00 a.m., to exercise. I have learned to carve out that hour for myself and not apologize for it. I rarely let something intrude on that hour—unless it's truly necessary. I am a better anchor and manager if I have that time for myself in the morning. The rest of the day is given to my work.

When I worked at the White House, I would get up at 4:12 a.m. My alarm was set for 4:20 a.m., but I always beat the buzzer, and I didn't want the alarm to wake Peter up. Those were tough hours, and I still get a sinking feeling whenever I have to get up in the 4:00 a.m. hour.

My point isn't to impress you with my early bird routines but to say I have learned to work in the hours when I'm most productive. I work well in the morning (so did President Bush, so we were a good pair). I can do well through 6:00 p.m., and then after that I have to push myself to stay alert if I'm on air (except for election nights, which are electric—no one could possibly fall asleep!).

Over the years, I've felt pressure from friends because my work has often made it impossible to carve out time for them. I am grateful for my understanding husband and family—their support is important. None of us needs to feel guiltier because we have demanding jobs and are ambitious in our careers.

I have a friend whose family often complains that she's so preoccupied with her work. "She's always busy!" they say. Well, she happens to have an important job and she's doing very well. She needs support, not more pressure from the people she loves. (She also needs a margarita, given some of her wild days at the office.)

It's important that we all give each other a break. If dinner plans get canceled, be okay with that. If someone can't make it to a birthday party, give them a break.

If you're always nearly drowning in work, then you have a responsibility to fix that. There are lots of tools out there—maybe you need to get up an hour earlier in the morning. Or maybe you need to approach your employer about getting some help to manage your workload. Do not be embarrassed about this. If you have a case to be made on the merits, they'd rather help than see you overloaded, or possibly even lose you to another company.

I recommend finding or inventing a new system to organize your day. We all get the same twenty-four hours—it's how we use them that sets us apart from others.

Working in television, I have very structured days. I know where I need to be and when—I can't ever run five minutes late. And that suits me very well. Every day I look at my calendar and see how much time is allotted per meeting or task—it gives me a road map for how I can fit everything in.

At the White House, the schedule is a thing of beauty—and of power! Whoever controls the president's time has a lot of clout. President Bush's days started at 6:00 a.m. in the Oval Office (though he was up at 5:00 a.m. to read the news and have coffee with Mrs. Bush). From there, each fifteen-, thirty-, or sixty-minute increment was spoken for. Even if that meant "personal time." As you get busier, you'll want to make sure to schedule time to clear your mind, exercise, meditate, walk the dog—whatever it may be.

If you don't work at the White House and don't need to be so hyperscheduled, you can find other tools that help you manage time, like Evernote and Todoist.

I suggest dedicating five minutes at the end of your workday to look at your calendar for the next day or two. See if there are conflicts you need to address the night before so that you aren't scrambling in the morning.

If you need to have a meeting with someone, try scheduling breakfast instead of lunch. Breakfasts rarely get canceled and end on time because everyone has somewhere they need to be. And eggs and bacon are less expensive than anything at lunch or dinner.

I also recommended cutting out a few things—even if you thought they'd help you get organized. I finally had to unsubscribe from *Real Simple* magazine because all of the ideas for how to make life at home easier were stressing me out! It was more like *Real Complicated* to me.

For example, if you don't really need to be at a weekly meeting, make the case to send someone in your place. If the book club meets too frequently and you can't keep up, ask if anyone else is feeling that way. Chances are that others are just as squeezed for time. Suggest meeting less often, or, if that's not a popular idea, just bow out for a few months. Remind yourself that there will be book clubs in the future—you may miss out on this particular experience, but there will be more.

Extracurricular activities are wonderful, but if they're hampering your ability to be successful at work, reevaluate what you're getting from each activity. Make some tough choices and focus on just one or two that really work for you. Ask yourself, Do I really need to learn the art of zen sand gardens?

I am not the best at saying no to invitations to speak at events, even if they are way out of my purview. So, I try to focus on three main areas—supporting veterans, especially through Canine Companions for Independence; charities with a focus on Africa, such as Mercy Ships; and Minute Mentoring. These are the organizations that make me feel that I'm being helpful to the causes I care most about. Narrowing it down to three allows me to put more energy and focus into them, which in turn gives me great satisfaction.

I've tried to follow the advice of one of my bosses at Fox News—that I can't do everything at once, and there are some things that you'll want to do later in life when you have more time. Even though I feel guilty when I disappoint someone, I do gain a sense of relief when I protect my time. I try to use words that soften the rejection: "I know you'll understand—your project is so important and they are fortunate to have you heading it up"; "I am honored you thought of me and hope that I can one day participate fully"; and "It might sound like I hung up, but I didn't, so keep talking…" (Actually, don't use that last one.)

Here's something to keep in mind: We all have more control over how we spend our time than we realize.

The tools are out there to better handle everything. You can do it. And once you have a little more white space in your calendar, protect it. Mark it as busy if you have a shared office calendar. No one needs to

know what you're doing for that thirty minutes if you've added meditation or a walk to your routine (or yes, even zen sand gardening).

Take control of the clock so that the clock doesn't take control
of you.

The perfect work–life balance revealed

Ha! Made ya look!

Everyone is looking for the perfect work-life balance. Let me tell
you something: it doesn't exist. The perfect balance is only whatever
you decide it is.

In every mentoring event I've ever done, this is the question that
always comes up. For some reason, people think that I have this figured out. I really haven't. I struggle with it, too.

I love to work. I thrive on it. So, I don't worry very much about a balance anymore. I realize that's not perfect, but it works for me. For now.

When I worked at the White House, there was very little balance. There was just no other way to put it. And it was hard to
describe. But at the Bush Center a few years ago, I heard a former colleague explain how she dealt with work-life balance, and it
changed my thinking about it.

She had a very important job in national security. Almost all her
waking hours were spent working, often in the Situation Room.

Over the five years she worked in the administration, she said she
missed almost all her friends' and family's birthdays, weddings, and
retirements. Instead of being full of regrets, she said she approached
it all knowing that it was temporary. She was likely never to work in
another White House. So, she thought about balance over the course
of her lifetime, rather than in her day-to-day life. And this gave her the
time she needed to dig into her career and do really important work.

Fast-forward a few years. After the White House, she wrote great books and taught at a university. Her schedule was more manageable, and she made up for lost time with friends and family. And she started a family of her own and is a happy working mother.

I thought that her approach was very good. Perhaps the way to think about work-life balance is to know that there will be times in your life—likely right now as you read this—when you need to put in more time at the office than you might want (or than your family might want). Remind yourself that it isn't forever—that there's a reason you're putting in this time now, because you want to get to a certain goal (to finish a project, earn more money, get that promotion), and that you'll have time on the other side for things like your hobbies or a vacation you've been wanting to take.

Beating yourself up for not having the perfect balance is pointless. And most successful people work more than they play for most of their lives. The goal should be to align your work with what you want to do so the reward is clear.

And technology gives us flexibility to work from anywhere—within reason—so utilize that when you need to. For example, can you take a conference call for a few minutes while your son warms up for his Little League game? Yes. But when he's up to bat or on the mound, that's the time you focus on being present and cherishing.

And if the work is really getting to you, then you have to make a change. I recently mentored a young woman who was very upset that her weekends were being taken up with work. Now, this was during the election year when, yes, if you're in the media industry, you're going to have to work weekends. After a while of talking it through, it was clear she wanted a change to a job that had more structured hours. If that's you, be glad! That means you've figured out what would work better for your lifestyle.

For the rest of your working years, you'll keep wrestling with finding the balance that works for you. Just keep trying—and pay attention to your reaction, to how you feel. If you do this—and think long-term—you will find your way to it.

To recap: Balance is in the eye of the beholder, and so is the power to find it. You'll have to make some tough calls—maybe you readjust and miss a dinner or two, staying home so you can rest and reset. Maybe you realize you need more sleep or more exercise or, sometimes, more *fun*. Remember you're a young woman—you'll be working for most of the rest of your life. You don't have to do everything all at once. If you try, you'll burn out and be set back. So pace yourself, take care of yourself, and be honest with yourself about what you need.

Namaste.

Wellness—you're in charge

To be your best, you really have to take care of your health. That means eating well (there's no shortage of information on the importance of cutting down on sugar and adding more vegetables to your diet), getting moderate exercise, and avoiding things that can lead to harm.

And if you have health insurance, then make sure you keep appointments for regular checkups and diagnostics. Catching problems early and prevention are the keys to staying ahead of any major health issues.

Former White House press secretary Tony Snow told me how he had put off his colonoscopy for nine months during a busy period when he was hosting a daily radio show and *Fox News Sunday*. His mother had died from colon cancer when Tony was young so he was in a special risk group that was supposed to get checked earlier than other men his age. Sadly, Tony was diagnosed with colon cancer and he fought it courageously for years. But in 2008, he succumbed to his illness.

Before he died, he made me promise that I would never put off my appointments, because he said that he always would wonder if he might have had a greater chance for survival if they had diagnosed it earlier. That really shook me. And to this day I have not ever skipped an appointment, even when it's inconvenient and there's a lot of news happening and I feel I should be at the office. I will never forget my promise to him. And I ask you to promise yourself the same thing. Be vigilant in safeguarding your health.

I recommend keeping a "doctor diary," as it can be hard to track what you've gone in for. For example, "March 2021—derm appt. All clear." That way you won't have to rely on your memory, and you'll be able to look back to see when you're due for another checkup.

Oh, final tip in this section: Sometimes I'm asked what is something I'd like to tell an eighteen-year-old version of myself. My answer: "Wear more sunscreen!" Seriously, you'll thank me later.

Risks and rewards

President Bush used to talk a lot about the need for Americans to be less risk averse. If you think about it, America was founded by people who took enormous personal risk to leave their home countries, bound for a new land and a new adventure. Many of them came with nothing and made new lives here through hard work. But they also had a strong tolerance for risk. Do you?

I am fairly cautious. I follow rules as much as possible. Okay, except for jaywalking, I have a perfect record. And then there was a highway robbery rap back in Colorado, but I beat that . . .

I don't go bungee jumping or ride rickety roller coasters anymore.

I'm a nervous car passenger (this drives Peter crazy—he says that I'm more likely to cause an accident because of my worries than if I just sat back and enjoyed the ride). And I don't even go whale watching because I am afraid the whales will come up and knock the boat over. (It happens!)

When it comes to work, I have sometimes been too cautious. I'll never forget joining a public relations firm when I left the White House—it was a safe choice. I knew as I signed the contract that it wasn't a good fit for me. And boy was I right! I needed more independence, and frankly, I could have made a lot more money being on my own rather than working for a firm.

Around then, I saw President Bush and his first question to me was, "What's wrong?" I said, "Oh, I'm fine..." But he knew me well. He tilted his head down and looked over the top of his reading glasses at me and said, "Spill it."

So, I told him what was going on in my post–White House work life and he said, "Why don't you start your own business?"

Well, at the time, I had a long list of reasons why that wasn't a good idea. I didn't have office space or a staff, I wasn't sure how to begin, didn't know how to get the resources or how I'd service the client if it were just me, etc.

President Bush was not persuaded. He said, "Ask yourself— what's the worst thing that could happen if you start your own public relations business?"

I thought about it. And I came up with some answers and he said, "Right. None of those sound like reasons to me that you shouldn't be your own businesswoman. You're telling me the worst thing is that the business fails and you have to go back to working for a different public relations company? That's the worst thing?"

Aha. He was right, as usual. President Bush quite likes career counseling, and I was fortunate to be mentored by him.

He pushed me to give it a shot, and I did. As he predicted, my business was successful. I was making more money than I ever had before. I hired two people and was on the cusp of needing another. By all accounts, everything was going very well.

But the truth was I didn't love it. I was working even longer hours than when I was at the White House, which was taxing on me and really frustrating to Peter.

Anyway, it didn't last too long—just as I was facing a decision about whether to hire more staff for my company, Fox News asked me if I'd be willing to co-host a show called *The Five*. Now, that was an easier decision for me. (They never mentioned the part involving Greg Gutfeld.) I very much wanted to do that. And I asked myself, What's the worst thing that could happen? The show doesn't succeed and I have to start my business up again? I'd already proven I could do that.

Every day you're faced with decisions—and there's a certain amount of risk that comes with all of them. Test the waters of what you can tolerate. You can often handle more than you think you can.

If you risk a little more and succeed, the reward is a little greater. And if you're an educated woman in America, well, all you really have to decide is how hard you want to work. If you're reading this, you've already made the decision that you want to succeed. To do that, be willing to take some risks.

Get comfortable with being a little uncomfortable.

Making your move

One January night in Washington DC, we hosted a Minute Mentoring session right before the State of the Union address. We called it "The State of You." During the panel discussion, we got a question from a young woman that really stumped us: When do you know it's the right time to leave a job? (Assuming, that is, you weren't fired.)

I fumbled around with some answers, but my experience had been that I'd left jobs because of greater opportunities. I'd never become bored or felt like I was underutilized before I had a new position. Then, Evan Ryan of Axios spoke up. She had the best answer.

Evan described how during the Obama administration she had worked for Vice President Biden in the intergovernmental affairs office, being the contact for all the mayors, county commissioners, and governors in the country. She said she loved that job, loved working for Biden, and when President Obama won reelection, she was quite prepared to keep doing what she had been doing in the first term.

Out of the blue, she got an offer to move to the State Department in a job she wasn't seeking and wasn't sure she could even do. She wasn't inclined to take it, but she said she'd think about it. She sought the advice of a woman she very much admired.

Her friend asked Evan if she felt like she was nearly drowning every day in her current job. Evan said absolutely not—she loved her job and was comfortable in it. And her friend said, "Then you have to leave. You need to feel that the waterline is just below chin level; you have to keep growing and grasping if you're to improve and reach your full potential."

As she finished this story, my co-panelists looked at each other and realized that was great advice. For me, when *The Daily Briefing* was added to my schedule and I was then doing two shows plus the podcast, I definitely felt like I was about to drown most days. And it was invigorating. Peter said he could tell I was thriving—and he was excited to see that in me.

If you've found yourself stagnating, not really challenged, and able to do the job with your eyes closed, maybe it's time to get going. You owe it to yourself to be moving up and out. That could mean within a company if you love it.

It could also mean going off to get more experience so that you can come back to a company that you love but where there isn't a growth opportunity in the cards. It's also a good time to consider starting your own business—remember to ask yourself, What's the worst that could happen?

Everyone I know who has taken the plunge to start a business has gone through a rough few months but then says they'd never go back to being an employee. Independence is self-reinforcing and confidence building.

Not too long ago, I was talking with a friend about her next career move. She was ready for a change, but after a year of searching, she just wasn't finding the right fit. At one point, she was offered a job that she hadn't even interviewed for. She had come highly recommended to a new executive. When she got the offer, her initial instinct was to decline. It wasn't in her plan, and it wasn't exactly what she wanted to do. But she thought it over. And we concluded that a transition job is a good thing to have sometimes, while you figure out what else you may want to do. It could turn out to be the perfect fit. Who knows? Maybe you'll enjoy bison ranching or professional wrestling.

I know that many people are worried about lateral moves. They think that doesn't show progress. But what if that lateral move leads to something else? Or if it doesn't, maybe it's a chance to learn a new skill and broaden your network. Accept opportunities because you are interested and you want to grow. Don't reject them just because you don't think they would look good on a résumé. One thing can definitely lead to another, and that can be very worthwhile.

My advice is to have your eyes and ears open at all times for new opportunities. Keep a lookout for yourself, your colleagues, and your friends. Remember my networking tips on making friends everywhere you go (from chapter 5, section 6). You will be more able to get on the calendar for informational interviews, where a chance conversation can lead to your next big thing. If I hadn't gone to that hockey game...

You may have no idea what you're capable of or how your skills could be useful to certain fields. I see this often with military veterans I chat with. After years as a soldier, sailor, or marine, they have a difficult time explaining how their skills on the battlefield can translate into a good job in the private sector.

I asked one female vet who was transitioning out of the military what she thought she was good at.

"I'm pretty good at blowing up stuff, keeping my mouth shut, and being there for my guys when they need me. But none of those things make sense on a résumé," she said.

I disagreed. Boy, did I disagree.

"Here's what I hear when you tell me your skills. Your experience blowing stuff up means that you'd be good at keeping stuff from getting blown up, like critical and expensive infrastructure, that you know how to keep a secret for sensitive projects, and that you're a reliable colleague. You sound like a great teammate to me!" I said.

Then I thought of three to five people I could connect her with, either by making an email introduction, setting up a time to meet for coffee, or getting her résumé to the top person at a place she'd want to work. I have a lot of connections—that's one of my strengths—and I use them to help others get connected. I may never see that person again, but they'll always know I was helpful when it mattered.

And if I ever need someone to help me keep something from blowing up, I know who to call.

Don't be afraid to move

Americans have long been the kind of people who will up and move to chase a new opportunity. Think of the pioneers, the gold rush, and the oil and tech booms. That's how we built the country and grew to be the largest economy in history. In the last couple of decades, the number of people moving for work has declined—but I'm here to encourage you to consider it. One of my favorite pieces of advice is "Don't be afraid to move."

First, I love an adventure. I like learning about a new town, getting lost in its history, and navigating my way around. I like meeting new people and making new friends. Fresh starts are invigorating.

I've moved a lot over the years and always for new opportunities (including for love when I moved to England). I've benefited from having so many different experiences. I have a good understanding of what makes different parts of the country tick, and I have many conversation starters because I've been to nearly every state in the country. (Except North Dakota—I swear I'm going to get there one day!)

I feel like I can pretty much fit in anywhere—I was born in Wyoming, spent the majority of my early career in Washington DC, had an amazing year in the United Kingdom, gave Southern California a whirl, loved the Lowcountry of South Carolina, and now call New York City and the Jersey Shore my home. All of this has served me well professionally and personally—I have friends every place I've lived.

One of my favorite stories about moving comes from former First Lady Barbara Bush. They'd been living in Midland, Texas, for a few years. She loved it. They had good friends, a strong, hardworking community, and a happy life.

Then one day, her husband, George H. W. Bush, came home from work—and announced he was going to go into the offshore oil drilling business. The problem was that Midland was way too far from the Gulf of Mexico, so they were going to have to move to Houston.

At that moment, Mrs. Bush decided to take her own advice, and in a flash, she chose to be happy. Instead of expressing her disappointment, she said, "Well, that's wonderful. I've always wanted to live in Houston!"

Eventually, Houston became the Bushes' beloved hometown. And it all started with a positive mindset of knowing that you can leave a place you love and find that same feeling in a different home. You have the power to do that—it's not always about the circumstances around you.

I find that a lot of young people who love living in New York City or Washington DC are very hesitant to think of living in a smaller midsized town, even if the career opportunity is very good. You might think that smaller towns are boring and backward. But if you visit, you'll find the people make a place—and that sometimes smaller means more chances to shine, more opportunities to grow, and even options for new business ventures or volunteer work. Even public service, like running for office, might be more possible in a smaller city. And as the saying in New York goes, "Sometimes you have to move out to move up." (There's also another saying in New York these days about the mayor. I'll spare you.)

So, if your company tells you that they have a promotion for you in Topeka, Kansas, don't wrinkle your nose right away. Sleep on it. Try saying, "Well, that's amazing—I've always wanted to visit Topeka!"

Make the most of your unexpected opportunity (and negotiate a great salary—build up some capital, buy a home, put yourself on a stronger financial footing). And then you might find that you really like it. Or you won't.

Just remember—and I tell myself this all the time—you are not stuck. You are an American woman—free to make decisions and to try and fail and to try again and succeed. It might just take you a while to get there. But enjoy the journey—build up some road underneath your feet. It will carry you farther if you do.

Now, I realize there are a lot of people hesitant to move or who don't have any wanderlust. Home is a great place (I feel the tug, too—when I visit the Rocky Mountains, I think, *How could I have ever left?*).

Plus, family is important to a person's well-being, too. I know that there are pulls and often pressures to stay—families don't want to see you go. But that can be overcome, and technology allows people to be in much better touch than ever. I realize that some parents rely on family to help with childcare, and my suggestion to be open to moving has to be weighed against other considerations. I get that.

I recently had to catch myself because a particularly good younger friend of mine was under consideration for a great new job, and I was thrilled for her . . . until I realized the job was in California. I said, "Oh, but maybe they'd let you do that job from New York," and she caught me. She said, "You'd be the first one to tell me not to be afraid to move." She was right. I was being selfish. I'd miss her so much that I was already putting more pressure on her rather than just saying, "That's amazing and I will visit and we'll still talk all the time and this is going to be great."

We have to encourage each other. Even if that means that we are a little sad about the parting of ways. Besides, you can always come back (please come back).

When in doubt, do the right thing

Integrity is extremely valuable. Maybe invaluable. It is the way you conduct yourself, even when people aren't looking. I've been very fortunate to surround myself with people of great integrity, at work and in my personal life. Integrity ensures that people can trust you, that you don't make decisions based on what's popular but rather on what is right. It's following your instinct on doing the right thing. It means you live by a code of decency, where you protect yourself and your company from unnecessary harm or bad decisions. It's how you're able to stand up for people when they've been wronged, and it's a way to stick up for yourself, too. I believe that everyone has the ability to live a life of great integrity—but they have to actively choose to do so.

You have to cultivate it so that it's your default. Do this, and you will always have that "last line of defense" inside to guide your decisions. Plus, you will never have to look over your shoulder—or worry about your name appearing in an uncomfortable Instagram caption.

If you feel your integrity is threatened, you have to stop before you do anything. Don't act before you think things through. Save yourself. Think back to the introductory story at the beginning of this book—the young woman who was concerned she was being put in a position to say something she didn't feel comfortable saying. She was worried enough that she reached out to me for advice. Trust those instincts. They will serve you well.

Clutch in a crisis

Being a levelheaded person that's good in a crisis is a valuable asset. Leaders look to promote people who are calm, collected, informed, and able to execute a plan to manage the problem. Screaming, "Oh Jesus God!" in the office when the pressure hits will do little to advance your career.

You might not know how you'll perform in a crisis until you're in the middle of one. It isn't something you can practice, unless you're able to take part in drills (and if those are happening at your work, volunteer to be a part of them).

What you can do in the meantime is give some thought to how you will respond when an emergency happens. Can you be someone that people turn to in a crisis?

Someone that people look to for help? Or are you the person they send for coffee?

You can study crises from the past to learn about how organizations handled a major problem; for example, I recommend reading about how in 1982 Johnson & Johnson tried to reassure the public after someone tampered with several bottles of Tylenol by putting cyanide inside. Seven people died from taking what they thought was Tylenol. No one was ever charged or convicted in their murders. To prevent a panic, Johnson & Johnson had to move swiftly.

First, the company took all Tylenol products off the shelves, out of an abundance of caution and at considerable cost. The executives were clear about what they knew and didn't know (people appreciate candor). They also expressed sympathy for the victims. And they immediately moved to tamper-resistant bottles. There's much more to it than my summary, but trust me that to this day, Johnson & Johnson's management of that crisis is considered the gold standard.

There are many more examples, and the more you read about them, the more you'll be ahead of the game for when you are part of a crisis management team.

I was part of such teams during many crises at the White House. One of them was Hurricane Katrina. The storm was wicked, but the aftermath was even worse—many people suffered from the heavy rain and strong winds, but many more endured hardships because of the lack of a good coordinated response by the government.

Frances Townsend, the White House homeland security advisor, handled the after-action report about Hurricane Katrina. She was blunt in her criticism for where the intergovernmental response failed to coordinate to protect people from harm (the local decision not to evacuate New Orleans and the surrounding area being the most important).

She also pointed out what needed to be improved, including ensuring more supplies and equipment for health-care workers and clearer communication to citizens about the resources available to them. Ever since this report, with its concrete recommendations, the intergovernmental response has been much better.

If you go through a crisis at your workplace, consider heading up an after-action report for the company. Gather information about what worked and what could be improved. That way you'll have something to go back to that will help the organization handle problems better in the future.

Employers are always looking for people with good crisis management skills. Keep that in mind when you interview—use these stories as examples of work that you were proud of.

Here are a few of the steps I try to follow in any crisis:

- Listen.
- Write down what is known and unknown.

- Speak softly. Slow things down. Others will sense your calm and feed off of it.
- Ask how to best get answers to what is unknown.
- Delegate tasks to get more information.
- Step into a role if there's a leadership vacuum—shoulder more of the burden if you can.
- See how you can support the top decision maker. What information do they need? Can you help provide it?
- Write clear statements that provide concrete information for the team.
- Keep a goal in mind—getting through the next hour, the next day. Create tasks that are manageable for you.
- Stay out of the way if you're not needed (this is important).
- Save the blame game for later.

Crisis management is a valuable skill that will serve you well. You never know when you'll need it.

Be the difference

If you've ever been to a retirement party, you've heard some of the tributes and toasts to a person who is finally making that tough choice to retire and enjoy other pursuits. These are motivating events, especially when you hear their former employees or colleagues tell a story from when the retiree taught them a lesson, inspired them to do better, or got them to step up.

I always wonder, *What might they say at my retirement party?* (I hope it's not, "Oh, thank God.")

I was thinking of this while talking to a friend who works in banking. He manages the young associates as they embark on a two-year program that is very competitive. If you do well, you could get a permanent position with a terrific company that pays very well.

He was telling me about this young man from Mexico City who got into the program. He said he was very likeable and charming, and he did an okay job at the tasks in front of him. This young guy had a lot of confidence. He thought he was doing great! But his cockiness didn't match his performance. He was not going to be destined for greatness with the company unless some changes were made.

When it was time for a check-in, the young man came in all smiles, expecting a good report. Instead, my friend asked him to sit down and explained that if he didn't improve, he'd not get a job and he'd be heading back to Mexico City without a good reference from the bank. The young man was in shock. But instead of protesting, he immediately asked, "What can I do?" And my friend gave him some specifics.

To his credit, the young man turned everything around, sharpened his pencils, and got to work. Within a year's time, he became vastly more capable.

And I guarantee that at my friend's retirement party, this young man will tell that story and say that moment made the difference for him.

So even when you have to deliver bad news or be tough on someone, know that it is likely to make them perform better, and they'll never forget that you gave them a chance to improve.

Resolution you

The week leading up to New Year's Day is one of my favorites. Not because of the parties—I know none of you thought that was why!

Rather, I quite enjoy the contemplative period to assess the year that's ending and to get excited for the year ahead. Goal setting is important, especially as you're starting out in your career and have plans to move up.

I suggest writing your goals down in one-year, two-year, five-year, and ten-year increments. Visualize what you want. And think big.

Do you want to argue a case in front of the Supreme Court? Advise a president? Run a start-up with a big team of excited young people? Travel the world on business? Have enough vacation time to take your dream trip—or to volunteer on a mission?

Allow yourself to imagine what it takes to make that happen. Set that intention, then make a choice: How hard do you want to work? That is in your hands. Decide well!

I suggest making a few lists that assess your strengths and weaknesses: Where do you stack up well? Where do you need to step it up? What are the things that can be addressed immediately? What are the toughest things you need to tackle? And then write out some ways that you could start to improve. Writing it down makes it feel a little more manageable.

Keep in mind that there is a difference between planning and dreaming. Give yourself time to daydream, to imagine what you might achieve in the future, what your life could look like. Use your imagination. Let your mind wander and suddenly you might come up with a way to solve a problem.

I also recommend sharing your goals with a couple of trusted friends, a mentor, or even your boss. If they don't know where you want to go, they won't be able to help you. And they can help keep you accountable by checking in on your progress.

Putting it all together

The more advice I give, the more things I remember that I picked up over the years. You'll be the same way when you're at the height of your career. Some ideas may save you time; others may save you money. All of it will help you manage life better and make success more likely.

It usually takes three weeks of practicing a new habit for it to stick. Take the ideas that work for you and run with them. As Michele Chase said, you just have to do it. Don't accept excuses for yourself; instead, lead by example, show people (and yourself) that you can learn new skills, improve your career trajectory, and be on that path to being able to ensure that everything will be okay.

You're well positioned. You want to succeed, to be excited about your life, and to be peaceful and happy. Now you have more tools to help kick your career into higher gear.

These habits will get your work life on the right track. The next piece of the puzzle? Addressing your own happiness. It's easier than you might think. Turn the page on your new outlook. (And also, literally turn the page!)

To recap: You're at the point in your life when you're starting to emerge from an entry-level position to one with more responsibility. With that comes more opportunity, challenge, and money. It also likely comes with longer hours and more stress. Start to set yourself up for success by employing this advice: take care of your health, pace yourself, and set clear goals so that you know where you want to go (and so that your boss can help you get there). This is an exciting time in your life—embrace the change!

〜〜〜〜

CHAPTER 7

Serenity: How Can You Detox, Recover, and Find Peace?

During the holidays in 2019, Peloton, the spin company, ran a commercial showing a husband buying his wife a bike for Christmas. Far from being angry that he got her exercise equipment for her present (the nerve!), she fell in love with the bike and rode it every day. She was glowing! The advertisers knew what they were doing. Women everywhere started putting "Peloton" on their wish lists.

Not everyone was so moved. Some people—on social media, of course!—took offense to the ad, saying that the husband was fat-shaming his wife, worsening body image problems for women. Okay—that's one way to take it. (A stupid way, I know.)

I had a different view. First, it's just an ad, people! Second, maybe she wanted the bike and was thrilled her husband had gone to the effort to make her happy. This is a tried-and-true way to sell products—even things like vacuum cleaners and leaf blowers! (Don't even think about it, Peter.)

All the talk about the Peloton ended up working on me, too. We got one that winter—after confirming with each other that it had nothing to do with hints about losing weight!

The bike became indispensable for me, especially as the coronavirus pandemic shut down gyms and required staying at home for quite a few months. I got much-needed cardio exercise without leaving the house, burned off a lot of stress, and had fun singing loudly to songs from the '80s (Jasper is now an Abba fan).

I love how positive the instructors are—cheerful, encouraging, and funny. One of the teachers, Hannah Marie Corbin, regularly reminds riders to adjust their posture for better comfort and alignment. She'll ask a series of questions:

What can you lengthen?
What can you tighten?
What can you soften?
What can you let go?

Those questions helped me get through my rides—I'd sit up taller, relax my jaw, and ignore my mental to-do list.

Her questions gave me an idea—could I use the same questions to take stock of my outlook and performance at work and at home?

So, I started thinking about how questions like that might help me during the day:

What can I do to be more present in the moment?
What worries can I let go?
How can I help calm tensions with my commentary on air?
Could I soften my attitude, words, and approach?

I'd repeat these questions to myself as I walked to work or when I folded laundry or while I was in the shower—any time I could let my mind wander.

Thinking about things that I could do to improve my days put the responsibility where it should be—on my shoulders. I've learned that despite really wanting someone else to improve my attitude and help me feel better, that's never going to happen. My family, friends, and co-workers certainly help me get through life, but ultimately it was important for me to learn the lesson that no one is going to save me.

This is true for you, too. Choosing to be happy, to be peaceful, to be loved—that really is up to you. You're in the driver's seat—now, which way are you going? (And as helpful as she can be, Siri is not available for this one.)

While I love excitement and adventure, the state of mind I crave the most is serenity—that feeling of being even and balanced. Alert, steady, and solid. That's what serenity means to me. It is not a passive feeling, but an energizing and inspiring one.

When I am in a serene state, I do my *clearest* thinking and my *best* work. It allows me the brain space to dream bigger and be more ambitious. And from a foundation of serenity, I can push myself in the right direction to attain my goals. To me, serenity ensures success. That's why I believe it is so important for you to discover what serenity means to you, too.

Finding serenity can be difficult—there are so many things that can block us from getting to that state when we're natural worriers. Sometimes it feels like it's you against the world instead of you *with* the world.

But there is a way to be serene more often. You need to identify what's eating you, getting you agitated, or keeping you up at night.

What would your version of my Peloton questions be?

Are you too uptight? Too frantic? Not motivated? Angry? Despondent?

In this chapter, we'll talk more about figuring out how you want to live. This is an important part of my discussion with anyone who comes to see me for advice. In almost every mentoring meeting I have, there's an elephant in the room. While it's usually the *last* question I'm asked, it's the *biggest* question on their minds: How can you find a way to be more settled and satisfied, relaxed and happy, while also pushing hard to achieve your goals?

Here's what I've taken away from those sessions. Aside from an improved job experience and a clearer upward trajectory for your career, you want

- to find some inner peace,
- to be more satisfied with your life's direction,
- to embrace your ambition while also being able to have valuable and sustaining relationships,
- to have a softer approach to treating others while not being a pushover, and
- to bungee jump off Royal Gorge Bridge in Colorado (not really).

Those goals are *100 percent* achievable.

Step one—the cleanse (but without any kale juice!).

Detoxify your mind—so fresh and so clean

How do you know if you need a detox? One thing to do would be to create an energy and emotion checklist—what are your answers to questions like these?

- Am I getting enough nutrition to sustain my health and support my mental and physical output?
- Are my sleeping habits helping or hurting my productivity?
- Do I feel exceptionally angry or close to tears over little things that should not elicit such a negative response?

- Am I so stressed that I feel close to physical or emotional burnout?
- Have I considered kicking people in the shins? Hard?

I'm sure that all of us could improve in these areas—we're human, after all!

I wish there were a pill or a tea that would do the job of a mental and spiritual cleanse for us. (And no—kale and beets don't do it. Even if they're blended into an eighteen-dollar juice.) Although Fortnum & Mason's Darjeeling may come close, alas, there is no such magical product. The only way to find more serenity is to clear your heart and mind of what's troubling you.

The good news is that there are many ways to have better answers to those questions. You get to choose how to do this.

I will leave it to you to address any physical cleansing you might need to consider and to seek help if you need it. Toxins come in a lot of forms—too much alcohol, sugar, tobacco, drugs, tech devices, and even exercise. Some of these can lead to addictions, and I encourage you to get professional help if you need it. If you're suffering in some way from substance abuse or mental illness or both, you're not expected to handle that on your own. There are professionals who are trained to help you—and they want to help. The first phone call asking for help might be the toughest act for you—but once you do that, you'll be on the path to recovery. Picking up the phone is a choice, too. That's the first step to getting well.

Toxins can also build up in other ways, too. For me, it used to be through worry. Rote worries cycled like a loop in my head from when I was a kid until...well, I think it basically ended when I left the White House. I'm not sure Peter would agree with that, as I did plenty of worrying when I finished in the Bush administration and was trying to figure out what I was going to do "for the rest of my life." (So needlessly dramatic!)

Now, at this stage in my life, the toxin I avoid the most is negativity. I have a physical revulsion to it. With friends who tend to be negative, I limit my contact with them and stay distant. It's either that or risk getting caught in their trap. I worry about how other people will feel about how they're treated. It's like I'm on constant high alert for it.

Another way that I can get all balled up with worry is that my entire life I've been conflict averse (and yes, I realize the irony that I work in cable news!). Ever since I was a kid, any sort of anger or frustration makes me so uncomfortable. Discord distresses me.

And I found that rage and anger, which are natural emotions at times, diminish me. I try to avoid them at all costs. Since it's not a comfortable state for me to be in, I am constantly trying to find the opposite of that. I spend an awful lot of time finding and preserving serenity. It's my quest—and for those moments when I find it, I find I can breathe and feel like everything is just as it is supposed to be.

The toxic buildup, however it manifests for you, is bad for your body and mind. If you don't actively flush it out of your system, it just keeps building up over the years. You might not even realize that it is weighing you down, suffocating your growth, and stifling your career or relationship.

How do you recognize when you have built up toxins that are harming you? Well, think about how easy it is for you to get angry or frustrated. Do you think that everyone is stupid, or that they're all working against you? Do you have crippling pangs of doubt? Do you constantly compare yourself to others? How easily are you moved to tears? Are you smiling right now because we've stumbled onto something?

Rest assured—if there's one thing I've learned, it's that you're not alone. At all.

As a reminder, if a peaceful mind is the goal, here's the most important prayer to commit to memory—it's called the Serenity Prayer.

> Dear God,
> Please grant me the serenity to accept the things I cannot change,
> The courage to change the things I can,
> And the wisdom to know the difference.

This simple prayer has been powerful for millions of people around the world, including anyone who's been a part of Alcoholics Anonymous. You can find this prayer hanging on walls, sewed onto pillows, and printed on T-shirts. Many books have been written about the power of this prayer, including *The Way of Serenity: Finding Peace and Happiness in the Serenity Prayer* by Jonathan Morris.

When I was growing up, we had the Serenity Prayer framed on our wall. I read it every day. And I've benefited from the prayer's message. If I get very worried, worked up, or find myself unable to sleep, when I remember to say this prayer, I can instantly calm down and be more rational and logical about what's bothering me.

Dana makes a list . . . again

So, with that as our goal, what's the first step to getting there? Identifying what it really is that's bothering you.

Let's start with a list. (Not with the lists again! Yes, one more.) I learned to do this when I was in college and have passed the practice on to those I've mentored over the years.

First, take a piece of paper and make three columns.

In the first column, write down all the problems, worries, and concerns you have. Make it as long as you want. Get it all out.

Title the second column "something I can change" and the third column "something out of my control." Then go down your list and mark them accordingly.

From the second column, evaluate the things you can change and brainstorm how you can solve the problems. Once you begin writing, sometimes it can be hard to stop. There might be several ways to tackle an issue that you hadn't been able to think of when your mind was cluttered. Just the simple act of writing things down will help you begin to solve the problem.

For the third column, the things that you can't change, you have to admit that you have no control. Surrender to it. Of course, that's a lot easier said than done, because those things are usually the crux of what you're worried about (a family member's addiction, a friend's divorce, or a colleague's illness).

I recommend reading over all the items in this column, accepting them as being things you cannot change, and then letting them go. You can visualize putting them into a bubble and letting it float away.

In Alcoholics Anonymous, they use the phrase "Let go and let God." It's at once empowering and freeing. But it isn't easy. Sometimes you'll have to go through this exercise quite a few times before you feel better—but I promise that it really can work. It helps you get to that point of realizing everything is going to be okay.

Take a while to let all that sink in. You might be surprised how many things you've been worried about that you have no control over. So, when you have this list, you now have a plan, or at least some ideas of how to handle problems that are bothering you, and a visual representation of all the things you can't do anything about.

Those are the things you can let go of and turn over to God or to the universe, however you think about it.

I recommended carrying this document around with you, especially if your worries are so overwhelming that it clouds your thinking and makes everyday tasks difficult to complete.

I did this once when we lived in San Diego. Peter and I had just moved there. He was starting a business, and I was looking for a job. We didn't have a lot of money, and while I knew I'd get a job doing something, I worried. *A lot.* Like, the "I'm forgetting to breathe" kind of worry. It was taking over my ability to think straight. Finally, at wit's end, I did the three-column exercise. Instead of throwing it away, I carried it around in my wallet.

One day at the supermarket, I felt very anxious, going over all the worries in my head again. I was stuck in the cereal aisle, staring at the boxes but not thinking about making a purchase. I was just a bit overwhelmed—maybe having a minor panic attack. (The choice of cereals these days can do that to you.)

Thankfully, I remembered the piece of paper—I got it out and read it in the cereal aisle, saw the things that were in my control and what I was doing about them, and all the things I couldn't do anything about, and I immediately felt better. Seeing that all my worries were there and accounted for, and that I had a plan for dealing with anything that was in my control, helped calm me down and get on with my grocery shopping. I even remembered to get Peter his Count Chocula.

There have only been a few times in my life when I've gone to the list in my pocket for emergency panic moments (fortunately, never on the air!). But every time I have, it's worked for me. And I hear good results from others who have tried it, too.

Be mindful of what your worry triggers are—is it change of any kind, relocating, yearly reviews, weddings, family get-togethers?

Whatever they are, if you know them well, you can be proactive in trying to manage your anxiety beforehand. And there are a lot of triggers—people, places, and things—as they say in the twelve-step world, so be really aware of these and try to look around corners for them so you're not caught off guard.

I used to get very anxious about being invited to baby showers. I really disliked going to them. I'd decided that I didn't want to have children of my own, and that was a personal choice that I didn't go around talking about. I considered that a private decision that Peter and I had made together. But inevitably, someone at the party would ask me if I had kids. I would say no. And they'd get a look of sadness for me, as if the reason I didn't have children was because I couldn't conceive. "I'm so sorry," they'd say. It made everyone uncomfortable. And a baby shower isn't really the place you want to explain why you decided that having children wasn't for you and your husband. (Remember the part about wanting to kick people in the shins?)

It got to the point that every time I was invited to a shower, I would dread it. Not only were there awkward conversations, but I also didn't want to play baby-name games and sit there while all the gifts were opened. And the last thing I wanted to be part of was some silly "gender reveal" that could lead to destruction of property. (Just get a cake, people!) I felt out of place.

I started finding or making excuses about why I couldn't attend (but I'd always send a gift—usually a few books that I loved as a child).

Then, suddenly, my little white lies caught up to me. I had used a presidential event as a reason I couldn't make a shower, and the host said that they'd change the date for me.

"We really want you to be there, so you give us what works for your schedule, and we'll work around that," she said.

I was busted.

I had to face a decision. Did I want to be anxious and resentful about the invitation or could I find a way to get out of it gracefully? I knew if I went, I would be miserable. But telling them I didn't want to go made me feel awful, too.

As I thought about my predicament, I was in a staff greenroom while President Bush was giving a speech. He got to a part in the speech about how it's easier to make decisions if you're guided by your principles, if you live by a code. I'd heard that speech several times, but this was the day it really struck me. I lifted my head. I had my answer on how to handle the baby shower invitation. I decided not to go. And I took it a step further. That day, I established a personal policy for myself that I do not attend baby showers. Making that decision, having that red line that I would not cross, made everything seem a little easier.

I called my friend. (By the way, pick up the phone to deliver news someone doesn't want to hear—don't just email or text. That runs the risk of coming off more negatively than you want. The right thing to do is to call. Make this a new principle for yourself!) I was honest with her, and she was so understanding. I remember she laughed and said, "Dana, it's fine. Besides, no one really likes these things!" (*So it isn't just me*, I thought.)

Her acceptance of my new policy meant so much to me. Of course, they wouldn't have invited me if they knew that I felt uncomfortable attending.

And now my policy was in the *Dana Perino Handbook*, and everyone seemed to get it. After I'd established my red line, I'd still get invitations but with an added note that said, "PS: We know you have a policy; we just wanted to make sure you knew you were invited."

Let me say I really love kids. I love babies. I love watching my friends become mothers and fathers. I will even babysit! But baby showers—they're just not my bag. So, my policy against going to baby showers is just a deal that I made with myself. It allows me to have better control over my time, and I don't have to fib. Plus, I still send a gift!

I've used the policy-creation exercise a few times. It includes getting home before midnight on New Year's Eve, not eating dinner after 8:00 p.m., and carving out at least an hour of exercise for myself every day. All my colleagues and friends know these policies—it makes for less peer pressure and a happier me.

Is there something that triggers your worst feelings that you can make a policy about to help you manage it?

I have a friend who will only agree to one weeknight event per week. She sticks to this rule and that makes it easier for her to decline multiple invitations: "Thank you—I won't be able to make it as I'm already booked this week." She made this commitment to herself, her husband, and her daughter and feels more in control of her schedule and protective of her family time.

Another friend became fed up with her husband's boss who would call during their family dinner hour and on weekends. One day, she answered her husband's phone and said, "Actually, we have just sat down for our evening meal, and this is special time for our family. Is this urgent?" It wasn't urgent. And guess what? They never got another call during dinner again!

And still another friend has great advice that she gives to all the young women that work for her, especially the young moms. One of our colleagues was back at work after her maternity leave, and she was in the groove. She had a lot of responsibility managing a big show, and it was difficult for her to take an afternoon off. On Halloween, she rushed out of the office and ran to her young daughter's day care for the costume parade. But she got there a few minutes late. She'd missed it. Hot tears ran down her cheeks—that feeling many working moms get when they think they can't do anything well.

When our friend, in a position of management, heard about this, she called the producer into her office. She said, "You absolutely must take those days off, without apology." She said, "You are a whole person—and we need you to know we recognize that. So, don't miss the first days of school, or the Halloween parties, or the birthday parties. We need you to be there, too."

I can't tell you how much this meant to the producer. It gave her the permission she needed to follow her instincts. And her staff adjusted. That's also a part of becoming a manager—can your team handle things without you while you go see your daughter in her bumblebee costume? They better be able to do so! Or you need to work on that, as well.

I appreciate learning these tips from my friends. I take the ones that I think would help me and add them to my own rule book!

I've made being a "policy wonk" work for me. You can, too.

Sweat out the small stuff

Have you ever found yourself cursing under your breath, or sighing with irritation at every little thing that happens? Like when you stub your toe, or the hot water has run out, or you accidentally put salt in your tea, then you receive eighteen emails with annoying requests, hit your funny bone on an open door, get cut off by a jerk on the highway, have your heel stepped on by someone getting off the elevator, the overnight package doesn't arrive, you get a paper cut, the train is late, and . . . it goes on like that all day?

And the thing is you can be mad or irritated at every single one of those things. But they're not just happening to you; they're happening to everyone every single day. And if you start out mad about a little thing, I guarantee that's going to snowball. You'll end up coming off as a jerk in a meeting, snapping at your assistant, firing off a nasty email, tweeting something inappropriate, yelling at your husband, possibly screaming in your office with the door closed, or even, at times, giving your co-host a judo chop.

Do you see how this can take over your life? We all know people like this. The ones who are rude to waiters, angry about the traffic, enraged by a slight of any kind. They're not fun to be around. I avoid them like the plague. Besides, I believe that negativity like this—if it is coming from within—adds wrinkles to a face and pounds to a waistline. So, if happiness isn't your goal, try it for less lofty reasons instead!

There have been many times in my life where I had to check myself because I was being the complainer in chief. It is a most unattractive habit. No one wants to be around someone who is angry all the time for every little thing that happens in life (this is true at home and at the office—nothing makes for a toxic colleague more than this).

When I catch myself being this way, I get very embarrassed. Being in control of my emotions, and being pleasant and grateful, is my more natural state. I feel unbalanced when I am being negative, and so I take action to shake it off.

As with most negative feelings, deep breaths help cleanse the mind and lower the heart rate. Then I offer an apology to anyone who deserves one. Finally, I try to name three positive things that happened that day. Sometimes it's a chore. But either way, I reset the clock.

I have some reminders in my bathroom that I've had affixed to my mirror above my sink that help keep me grounded. They remind me to:

- listen more than I talk,
- speak gently when I do, and
- learn to flow with the river rather than always pushing against it.

Most days I read all three a few times while brushing my teeth. (Gotta be productive!) Other days I just glance at them and remember that these bits of advice have been very helpful to me. Sometimes during the day, when I'm getting irritated or riled up, I picture those words in my mind and I calm down. The advice has really worked for me. Tried and true.

I believe that learning to dispel negativity from my life— including the small stuff—has given me the balance and strong heart I need to be successful. It is probably one of the most important life lessons I've learned, and I'm grateful for it. I don't need to levitate or be one with the universe. I work in New York, not Hollywood. But I strive for a certain internal evenness, positivity...calm. (Serenity now! *Seinfeld* fans will get it.)

I call this Perspective with a capital *P*. On my trips to Africa, I've been reminded how fortunate we are to be in our situation—living in freedom, educated, rewarded for hard work, capable of traveling every couple of years to do a little part to help people who are living in dire poverty. It has helped me to get that perspective I need—it reminds me to live with gratitude and not with negativity.

Once you make this choice, it becomes clear how many people are living with a constant stream of little disappointments and grievances. Set yourself apart from that, and you'll have a lighter heart, better days, and sounder sleep. Cut that deal with yourself—to remember how lucky you are, comparatively.

Turn the annoyances into opportunities to be grateful. See how it feels to be a gentler person. Let the corners of your mouth lift, and allow your inner warmth to radiate from within you to the outside world. Embrace the freedom that comes from avoiding and deflecting negativity, and you'll immediately see an improvement in your life. People will want to be around you. They will like you more, but more important, *you* will like you more.

Don't fall into the comparison trap

My final suggestion for detoxing and resetting is to try to reduce the amount of time you spend comparing yourself to others. We do this naturally—we are constantly measuring ourselves against friends, colleagues, even celebrities. There will always be someone thinner, taller (and I mean, that's almost *always* in my case), richer, more liked, smarter, stronger, etc. than we are.

Remember earlier in this book when we talked about how we tend to think that other people are thinking about us when they're really not? That they're thinking about themselves?

Theodore Roosevelt is credited with saying, "Comparison is the thief of joy." Memorize that quotation. Start to live by it—and remind others about it, too.

To be happy for another's success adds to your well-being. Comparing yourself to others subtracts from your own happiness—it's one of the biggest reasons that we worry.

Comparing leads to anxiety. Focusing on what someone else has rather than what we have or on how to work to have more is self-destructive. Besides, you are a unique, special person. No one can compare to you. If you're caught up in worry about someone else's plan, you're taking away valuable energy to focus on your own plan.

This is especially true on social media. We all know that the

"perfect life" you see on a Facebook feed isn't reality. And yet…
we can still get sucked into pining after someone else's life—their
great house, their amazing vacations, their unbelievably cute kids
(or dogs!). They have the perfect life! Then you read they're battling
addictions, or suffering from depression that they've hid for so long.
So don't be fooled.

A way to break out of coveting another person's social media
existence is to start a habit like this:

One thing I love about living in the city is being able to be
around a lot of bustle. I like how so many different types of people
come together to make everything work.

But a couple of years ago, when I was walking to work, I noticed
that few people were making eye contact with each other. They just
rushed by in such a hurry. Are we really *so* busy that we can't connect with each other as humans (or even as New Yorkers, who are,
theoretically, humans)?

So, I started saying a little silent prayer for each person I made
eye contact with. They go something like, "May whatever you're
going through ease up on you for today…May there be peace in
your heart today…May you be safe and secure…May you know
you are loved and cared for by God." It was a helpful exercise that
has become a habit, and I think I'm better off for it. It certainly got
me out of comparing my bag to her bag and her coat to my coat and
her cool dog to my—Who am I kidding? No dog beats out Jasper.

And the more people you know who achieve something, the
more it adds to your success, because you know them and you can
celebrate with them. Let your circle expand as much as possible—
you're within the circumference. And then when you achieve something, everyone in that circle will be happy for you, too.

Converting worry into energy

During the coronavirus pandemic, I sat for an interview with the host of the *I Want Her Job* podcast. I had some time on my hands, and we didn't have to rush. We ended up talking a lot about how someone can appear to be handling life so well, and yet they can be racked with worry underneath.

One of the questions was about how I deal with performance anxiety—did I still get nervous when the lights and cameras turned on, or was that behind me?

I still have nerves, but I had learned to channel that energy into fuel.

You need energy to perform—if I'm not energized, my show is going to be boring and the viewer will turn the channel to a better option. It's actually a term that TV people use: "That woman has 'good energy.'"

But while the host and I talked, I realized that I'd taken this lesson a step further for many years but had not ever verbalized it.

Let me explain: Think back to when I was the White House press secretary. I was on high alert with high anxiety all day, every day. I didn't sleep with one eye open, but I didn't sleep much. I had so much to do, and I wanted to do it well.

Whenever I'd go to do a press briefing, I'd remind myself that even though I felt prepared, I'd better be on my toes. I didn't ever want to disappoint the president or let down the country. But I also never wanted the reporters to sense that I was nervous. While I was always overprepared, I had a level of fear that something would go wrong. I just squashed it way down so that no one could tell.

I was turning that fear into something I could use—energy that would help me perform well. I couldn't cower in my office and not brief the press—that wasn't an option. I had to get up there. I learned to push all that internal conflict *outward*. (I'm surprised I didn't blow the doors off the White House some days.)

It's the same when we are asked to speak at a corporate retreat or give a presentation on the new model of a product that's coming out, or when we're confronting a problem with a colleague or having a difficult conversation with our boss. Avoidance can work up to a point, but there comes a time when you have to act. And getting up the gumption to do something uncomfortable and challenging is where you take that fear and convert it to serve you rather than hold you back. It's how you stretch and grow.

You can do this, too. Actually, you probably already do in some way. You can rewire your brain to turn worries and fears into fuel (a renewable one, too!).

Here's a trick: point your emotions *at* someone.

Say you have to give a speech, and your supervisors will be there. You're nervous as can be. So, to convert that energy, that emotion, into something more positive, pick one person—maybe someone you don't like?—and channel your energy at her. Don't let that person beat you. Make all that churning in your belly something you project out at the room, toward your target. It's a psychological trick I've used at times.

The point is that nervousness and energy can eat you up if you don't release it. Experiment a little to figure out the best way to do it. (My recommendations are to start with exercise, writing, and meditation. Of course, crying into your pillow on occasion can be useful, too.)

All the feels

Should you hide your emotions at work?

I can argue it either way. For a long time, women were advised to keep their emotions in check at the office, so that they could seem more like men and be more likely to get ahead that way. (Despite the fact that I've seen plenty of men melt down at work. They have this thing about kicking wastebaskets...)

I think we are a bit past that. We all have emotions. And sometimes, they are powerful and need to be expressed. I believe that in today's workplace, there's more tolerance for expressing oneself.

I've cried at the office a few times behind closed doors or with a trusted friend. Sometimes, with as much pressure as all of us are dealing with, and the tough news we have to report, it can all get to be too much. I've appreciated the kind support from my colleagues when this has happened. We are there for each other—it's quite meaningful to go through tough times together.

Now, outside of work? I cry quite easily. Usually what brings me to tears is kindness. When people are good to each other, when they help, going the extra mile, it really gets to me.

My grandfather Leo Perino was like that—I'll never forget him letting the slash timber piles grow and grow because he didn't want to burn down the habitat that bunnies had found. He would also get teary when he talked about America. I remember being with him in Newcastle, Wyoming, at 4:30 a.m. in the early 1990s for the beginning of the annual summer cattle drive. (Yeah, you read that right. A *cattle* drive.) We had to wait for the train to pass so that we had a clearing to get the calves and their moms across to head up to the meadow in South Dakota. As we sat there, chilly in our jean jackets, taking in the scene, he said, "Look at all we have here. And how we all are in this together. This is a beautiful country. There's no better country than America, Dana." A tear rolled down his cheek. Making me cry a little, too.

Now, my grandfather's love of country is something that everyone might cry over. But television shows, movies, commercials, books? That's me. I cry a lot. Once, when I was on a plane to

Houston, a flight attendant asked if I was going to a funeral. I said, "No, I'm just reading a novel about a family having to deal with their father's early onset Alzheimer's." (*We Are Not Ourselves* by Matthew Thomas—I highly recommend it…but grab some tissues.)

I find that letting those emotions well up and spill over is quite cathartic.

And Peter and I have had arguments about it. (Okay, it wasn't an argument—but I won anyway. Just ask Peter. He said when he met me, he knew he'd met Miss Right. He just didn't know my first name was Always.)

We had been watching this Australian series on Netflix called *Offspring*. I love this show—it's a family comedy drama that is super quirky. The main character is an obstetrician in her thirties who is dealing with romance and professional problems and family drama. I believe her sister, Billie Proudman, and I could be best friends. At the end of each day, I couldn't wait to watch it—we went through the seven seasons in just a few months. (Peter says he put up with the show, but I know he loved it, too. Guys love chick lit and dramedies! He never cried, but apparently he kept getting something in his eye.)

Without fail, I teared up at least once per episode.

I'd notice that Peter would anticipate these moments, and he'd look at me all concerned, and in an "oh, isn't that sweet" kind of way. I wouldn't turn to look at him—I wanted to watch the show and I didn't want to be embarrassed that I was about to get emotional.

Since I knew he was looking at me, I'd stuff the emotions down, trying not to cry. Well finally, one night I'd had enough. I turned to him and said, "Please stop looking at me when I'm about to cry!" I knew I needed to let those tears out. (Peter actually only cries over soccer games—he calls them "football"—and, strangely, *Rocky* movies. The British are weird.)

He said he just thought it was so sweet. I turned all kinds of not sweet and said he had to stop it. We then watched the rest of the seasons without looking at each other—or cracking up if we stole a glance. (This actually turned into a joke—we'd start laughing instead of me crying. Win-win!)

My point is cry when it feels like you need to cry. I don't believe in holding emotions in. Humans need to express themselves. Now, if you find you're crying all the time, triggered by any little thing, and it's interfering in your relationships or your job, then you need to seek some professional help to get you back on the right track. You don't want to turn into John Boehner every time you work late or someone screws up your lunch order.

But if you want to cry while you drink wine and watch the Hallmark Channel, you absolutely should!

This, too, shall pass

Here's another tip to keep in mind—you've heard it since you were a little kid. "This, too, shall pass" is an important reminder, a mantra that can help you cope with whatever you're going through.

Everything changes, evolves, and, eventually, stops.

When you're going through a tough time, remind yourself that it will come to an end. No matter what it is. This can help you hold on and get it behind you. And remember: the game is long...

Now, this is also true for the good stuff. The good times can end, too. Sometimes they end and are replaced by another good thing. Though be on guard for the creep of resentment when the good thing starts to pass—as we've established, our brains are wired for worry—so the chemical reactions of happiness, love, and excitement are all something we have to enjoy and savor while we manage the anxiety that inevitably tries to get our attention.

That's why it is important to count your blessings, to live with gratitude, to try to hold on to the good feelings and turn them into happy memories.

And strive for the long view. Chances are your worst day would be one line in your biography, were it ever written. Remember that. Nearly all of it is "small stuff."

Because everything will always change. And that's okay, too.

My hope for you

What I want is for you to realize that you can find a healthier, happier, more enriching, and calmer life. That it is within reach—with just a bit of focus and effort, and a commitment to living a sweeter life, squelching the bitterness that can start to take over.

You can start fresh, even if you're in the same town, relationship, or job. Right now—if you choose—the slate is wiped clean.

With a few good choices, you can find that state of grace where you are steady under pressure, thriving in your success, and contented in your knowledge about your true purpose in life. You can be the person you admire.

Think about holding a look in your eyes that is inviting—that says I'm open, I'm listening, I'm interested...instead of someone who looks down and away and frowns like they don't want to be bothered. Soften your gaze toward others, and especially toward yourself.

You can be both happy *and* wise.

A lot of this chapter has been advice on life outside of the workplace, but not entirely.

Realize this moment in our country's history. We are now in a time when a woman's expertise and talents are sought after, valued, and praised—after so much pioneering work of working women of previous generations. Think of those immigrant women, some of whom lived their lives in sweatshops, working sixteen-hour days. Think how far we've come. At this point, women are succeeding across the board.

For example, women have surpassed men when it comes to college attendance and college graduation. Women are also earning the majority of doctoral degrees. These educational attainments are leading to increased salaries, though in some cases there's still a pay gap between men and women. You must stick up for yourself and make sure that wherever you're working, there's parity—and fight for it for others when you become a manager, too. Also, a slight majority of women are now the main breadwinner for their households. This means more financial responsibility and a need to more equitably split the household and childcare duties for a family.

This is an incredible moment. And yet I still hear young women worrying about their male counterparts getting ahead of them, of having it easier than they do. Well, they may have it easier, but the constant comparing might be holding you back. I advocate for letting these pre-resentments go. These obstacles and gender disparities still exist and we should be mindful of them, but don't let them rule over your life.

Women can be in the driver's seat—so step on it!

Be gracious with this power. Advocate for justice and fairness. Embrace self-reliance and adulthood. And remember that it doesn't matter what others are thinking about you—and the likelihood is that no one is really thinking that much about you. They are thinking about themselves.

I have a friend in the technology sector who is an incredible success story. She grew up very poor and in an extremely strict and conservative household. There was some physical abuse—she says it was really the only way her parents communicated. Her dad hit her mom, and her mom hit her and her siblings. "Hurt people hurt people," she said—it's a saying that was very true in her home. Thankfully, a teacher recognized her intelligence, intervened to get her into a different school that would provide her more opportunities, and made sure she had the uniform and supplies she needed so that her parents wouldn't object.

Through education she was able to get into college and eventually started her own technology company. She's recently expanded her company, hiring more employees and expanding internationally. A beautiful woman, she looked like she had it all. It would be easy to be envious of her.

What you couldn't see were the internal scars from her youth, which were difficult for her to overcome. She saw a therapist for years, taking charge of her self-care. She purged the negative upbringing from her adult life, forgiving her parents but cutting off communication with them. She keeps in touch with her siblings but doesn't allow herself to get drawn into the negativity that weighs them down.

My friend found serenity by taking charge of her mental health and well-being, and as a result, she could focus on expanding her business and breaking through barriers.

That freedom is there for you, too. Embrace it. Find energy in the peace and serenity that comes from being a vibrant, intelligent, and responsible young woman.

And there, in those pockets of calm, when the worries are crossed off the list for a bit—right there is where you're meant to exist.

Once you find those feelings, like my friend who took charge of her life, you'll be able to return to them again and again.

Happy, peaceful, and serene. And completely okay.

Epilogue

In January 2020, I took on the project of writing a book filled with work and life advice for young women. My first book, *And the Good News Is…Lessons and Advice from the Bright Side*, was published in 2015, and the mentoring advice in that book was still relevant. Readers often asked when I was going to write another one.

I was five years older, too. I would soon be in my late forties (gulp!). I was regularly giving a lot of advice to young professionals, and I wanted it all in one place. It was time for an update. Dana's Advice 2.0 (slight reboot required).

The year 2020 started out like many others—I was trying to stick to that year's resolutions (posture), making Peter and me some sort of soup (no queso!) while we watched football, and going to bed early with a good book, Jasper sleeping by my side. I blocked a few hours each Sunday to write, make lots of notes, and find ways to procrastinate (my closets have never been so organized).

At Fox News, we covered the impeachment hearings, the Democratic primary, the president's reelection campaign, and the State of the Union Address. The state of the union was strong. However, we would soon learn that the same could not be said about the state of the world's health.

A global pandemic that started in Wuhan, China, upended 2020.

And the hits just kept coming.

To protect vulnerable populations and not overwhelm our hospitals and first responders, President Trump and the nation's governors made the tough decision to shut down our red-hot economy. It was shocking, jarring, and scary. Many millions suffered—either from ill health, losing loved ones, or from the economic fallout of hardship that was no fault of their own. It was sobering and stressful.

Our hearts broke for workers who suddenly found themselves in the desperate situation of joining food pantry lines that stretched for miles so they could feed their families. We watched reports of nurses holding the hands of sick patients in nursing homes and hospitals and putting up signs in the windows or sending text messages to friends and family who couldn't be there. Their pain was almost too difficult to watch.

Fox News set us up to work from home in mid-March. I cleared my schedule. "Cancel everything!" became my new motto (along with everyone else's). No dinners, parties, lectures, speeches, weekends away, or vacations. My calendar had never looked so clean. I had no distractions or obligations outside of being home and getting my work done.

To my surprise, I really liked the chance to slow down and focus. The sudden change to working from home and being in quarantine taught me something. I had time to step back and reflect. And for the first time in my professional life, I felt like I could handle my workload and have a very enjoyable personal life. I was…balanced.

I realized that once again, as during my White House days, I'd allowed myself to get too overscheduled. I needed more time to rest and be quiet so that I could perform better at work and be a happier, more productive person. And having more time with Peter and Jasper with long walks after work and homemade dinners rather than ordering in or going to a restaurant was more satisfying. More like when I was a kid and we had family time every night, watching the news and settling into our evenings.

One afternoon on a panel over Zoom that I did about the election, the moderator described me as "powerfully calm." I took that as a major compliment. That's what I wanted to be—and that's what I had become to others. I was more centered and energetic than I'd been in a long time.

All the while, there was your generation, being hit with an incredible challenge—starting your careers and families with a strong job market at the first of the year only to see that crater by March. The floor was yanked from under you. If you kept your job and could work from home, Zoom calls were not the same as human interaction. It took a lot of effort to stay engaged with colleagues, some of whom you may never have met. Mentoring was difficult, as was figuring out how to climb the corporate ladder from your bedroom while hoping your dog didn't bark during your presentation to the boss. Moving up or moving on seemed impossible.

It was unfair. Life can often be. But there was nothing you could do about it. History found you, as Caitlin Flanagan wrote in *The Atlantic* in April 2020. And the way many of you reacted impressed me.

Out of necessity, you got creative. You started businesses—making masks, delivering wine (thank you so much), and developing apps that made people's lives easier. You volunteered and used your social media networking skills to amplify your efforts. You kept a good attitude.

There was no way around the pandemic. You had to go through it. And you were stronger, gutsier, and more capable than you realized. You not only survived, you thrived.

Remember that the next time you face challenges. Whatever tools and lessons you learned during the pandemic will always be available to you. You've learned to manage in a crisis. You are more resilient for having gone through it.

As I was choosing the cover of this book, I asked several young women for their take. One of them read the title out loud, saying, "*Everything Will Be Okay.* Gosh, I really needed to hear that."

She wasn't alone. It's one of the reasons I knew the title of the book before I'd even written it. I knew you needed to hear it as much as I sometimes did. I could see the anxiety on your faces; I understood what you've been going through. I went through it, too. Trust me—it gets better.

And beyond telling you everything will be okay, I want you to actually believe it.

Make it your motto, your mantra. Repeat it to yourself as you're walking your dog, on the subway riding to work, while you're waiting for your Seamless delivery (everyone is talking to themselves these days—it's okay; they won't think you're crazy). It is a soothing, universal phrase—watch moms and dads who reassure their children over and over, "It's okay. It's okay." Even Jasper knows and understands "It's okay" (of course, he also knows "treat" and "walk").

Eventually, you'll emerge from this stage of your life. You can manage your anxiety if you actively take it on. There's a lot of advice in this book you can use to get you to a peacefully energized place. And with that frame of mind, you can keep making solid base hits and the occasional home run in your career. You can be your most fulfilled self.

Remember what's important. It's not all about success, moving up the ladder, money, and status. I learned that lesson again during the quarantine, but it would be good for you, my reader, to learn it now.

As you strive for success, don't forget the really important things: family, friends, making good memories, and holding on to the special moments. If you do that, life can't help but be okay.

Now, go impress me again. The world needs your ingenuity, spunk, and big heart.

We're counting on you.

Acknowledgments

When you write a book about living with gratitude, the acknowledgments could be as long the book itself. Bear with me. There were so many people who helped me, and from the bottom of my heart, thank you.

My admiration abounds for my editor, Sean Desmond. Only he could convince me to write another book in an election year. What were we thinking? With his love of good writing and his great advice, he helped bring it all together at the end. And *Everything Will Be Okay* turned out to be the right book at the right time after all.

The team at Twelve has been at my side through three books now. They stand out in the publishing field—small and mighty. So glad to be a part of their world.

Bob Barnett is the guide who has helped me navigate my career since my days in the White House. He packs more work into twenty-four hours than anyone I've ever known. He is always available, and without him I'd be lost.

I owe a large debt of gratitude to Paul Mauro. Paul spends his days helping to keep all of us safe, and then he'd stay up late at night to mark up drafts and make excellent suggestions. He had great advice for young professionals, and he helped lighten the mood—so if you got a chuckle as you read, all credit to Paul. He came up with the subtitle, and I laugh every single time I read it. His wife, Joan McNaughton, cheered me on throughout the process. The way she carries herself through life is something we can all look up to.

Ingrid Henrichsen is my sister-friend. She can read my mind even from afar. She pushed me to be more open about my own worries and mistakes, which made the book more personal and meaningful.

Jennifer and Chris Doris read along as I wrote and provided some great examples, which I incorporated into the book. Jenn really needs to write her own book one day, trust me.

Steven and Elizabeth Law so earnestly and joyfully supported me, and their parenting of their two young professionals gave me ideas for the advice chapters.

Jared Cohen has provided a forum through which I've made incredible friendships that have been personally and professionally rewarding. Thank you for pushing me to stay in New York City.

Lauren Fritts's meteoric career path is something I've enjoyed watching. Thank you for so much material! And to think it all started on that trip across the country with the worst (and best) junk food we could find.

Chris Byrne, a former assistant of mine, was the first to read the drafts and provided smart input. He's also my biggest fan, and I'm grateful for that.

My team at Minute Mentoring has been terrific all these years. Thank you to Dee Martin, Jamie Zuieback, Caitlin Andrews, and Erin Landers. Erin used to work for me, and now we'll all be working for her one day.

I even looped Jenny Landers, Erin's mom, into being an early reader. I knew we had a hit when she asked if it was okay to send the draft to her three daughters (Yes!).

Fox News Channel is filled with people wo bend over backward to be supportive and encouraging. I am grateful to Lachlan

Murdoch, Suzanne Scott, Jay Wallace, Meade Cooper, Kim Rosenberg, Porter Berry, Scott Wilder, Irena Briganti, Tessica Glancey, and Hamdah Salhut. The feedback from some very talented young women at Fox News who I entrusted as early readers was particularly helpful—my thanks to Allison DeBlois, Amy Fenton, Erin O'Donnell, Adreanna Walsh, and Pam Wentworth.

Inspiration also came from my colleagues, including Martha MacCallum. The way she manages work and home life is very impressive—a model for us all.

Particular thanks to the executive producer of *The Daily Briefing with Dana Perino* and *The Five*, Megan Albano. Over ten years, I've watched her grow professionally while becoming a beautiful mother to two children. When I think about who I'd recommend young women look up to, Megan is the first that comes to mind. "Be Like Megan" would have been a great subtitle.

Michelle Frazzetta and JoJo Rodriguez perform magic every day in the hair and makeup room. They are artists, and they've become like family to me. They also handled the book cover photo shoot—thank goodness!

And thank you to *The Daily Briefing* team—I am in awe of how you put the show together every single day. You are deeply appreciated.

As the book went to print, *The Five* was in its tenth year. Not bad for a show we thought would be temporary. It's been a wonderful run, and I'm so glad we are still going strong. Thank you to the brothers I never had growing up: Greg Gutfeld, Jesse Watters, and Juan Williams. I especially appreciate Greg's teasing—truly!—and will always think of him as a writer first and a television host second. The writing comes first (see chapter 5). And my compliments to the chefs who produce *The Five* every day—thanks for putting up with us, especially Scott Sanders, my producing partner on the show (this guy's got talent!).

And *I'll Tell You What*, my weekly podcast with Chris Stirewalt, produced by Jason Bonewald, served as a great sounding board as I wrote through the pandemic.

Now, you've heard the advice that you should hire people smarter than you. Well, I did just that. Caroline Sherwood is my assistant, and I'm in awe of her range of capabilities at such a young age. She has an incredible work ethic, is incredibly meticulous, and takes on every new project with enthusiasm and then handles them with such ease. She's a marvel. And a pleasure to work with. I'm so glad she's part of the Dana Perino Network.

Melanie Dunea is an incredible photographer and has taken the pictures for each of my books. She makes everyone look like their best selves.

Thank you to my secret weapons, Colin Reed and Matt Whitlock. Well, not so secret anymore!

Thank you to Emily Schillinger for your friendship, and for sharing one of the most inspirational stories not just of this book but of all time.

I also want to extend my thanks to President George W. Bush, who gave me the chance of a lifetime to serve as the White House press secretary. So many of the anecdotes in this book come from that experience. He set the perfect example for me. Perhaps the most important lesson was that we may have stressful days, but we are always joyful. Yes sir, we are!

My mom, Janice Perino, and her friend, Barb Weber, did a final copyedit of the manuscript and told me how they wished a book like this one had existed when they were starting out. They are part of the generation that paved the way for all of us, and we all appreciate that.

My sister, Angie Machock, is the family favorite, and for good reason. Thank you for your support, and for the laughs. And for your husband, Ben, for keeping you so happy. Oh, and the essential oils for my aching shoulders. I'm getting used to the scents.

My dad, Leo Perino, helped set me on this path, and I will always be grateful that he made me read two papers before he got home from work so that we could discuss them before dinner. Talk about setting me up for success!

I write so much about Peter in this book that I feel like you know him well. The guy is... beyond. I love how he suggested that every man should read this book—so that he can understand that he'll never understand women, but that he should always keep trying. Thank you for being you, Peter... and for being mine.

Jasper—thank you for lying next to me all those weekends during the shutdown while I wrote this book in Bay Head, New Jersey. I love it when you lay your head on my shin bone, and even though it hurts like mad, I won't move to avoid disturbing you. You're such a good boy. The very picture of happy serenity.

About the Author

Dana Perino is a Fox News anchor, a co-host of *The Five*, an analyst for Fox News election coverage and specials, and the #1 *New York Times* bestselling author of *And the Good News Is...: Lessons and Advice from the Bright Side* and *Let Me Tell You About Jasper*. Perino is the former White House press secretary for President George W. Bush, where she was the first Republican woman to hold the job. She served for over seven years in the administration, including at the Department of Justice after the terrorist attacks on 9/11. Perino grew up in the Rocky Mountain West and now lives in Manhattan with her husband, Peter McMahon, and their dog, Jasper.